the
FRAZZLED
FEMALE

Finding Peace in the Midst of Daily Life

Cindi Wood

LifeWay Press®
Nashville, TN

ISBN 978-0-6330-9526-0
Item 001238297

Dewey Decimal Classification: 248.843
Subject Headings: STRESS (PSYCHOLOGY) \
MENTAL HEALTH \ WOMEN

Art Director: Jon Rodda
Cover Illustration: Karine Daisay

Unless otherwise noted, all Scripture quotations are taken from the
Holman Christian Standard Bible®, copyright © 1999, 2000, 2001,
2002, 2003 by Holman Bible Publishers. Used by permission.

Scripture quotations identified AMP are taken from
The Amplified New Testament © The Lockman Foundation
1954, 1958, 1987. Used by permission.

Scripture quotations identified NIV are taken from
The New International Version © International Bible Publishers
1973, 1978, 1984. Used by permission.

To order additional copies of this resource:
WRITE LifeWay Church Resources Customer Service;
One LifeWay Plaza; Nashville, TN 37234-0113;
FAX order to (615) 251-5933; PHONE (800) 458-2772;
ORDER ONLINE at *www.lifeway.com*;
E-MAIL *orderentry@lifeway.com*;
or VISIT the LifeWay Christian Store serving you.

Printed in the United States of America

Leadership and Adult Publishing
LifeWay Church Resources
One LifeWay Plaza
Nashville, TN 37234-0175

Contents

Cindi Wood

Cindi Wood is an author, speaker, conference leader, and founder of Frazzled Female Ministries. She presents her Frazzled Female seminars for Christian women at luncheons, retreats, rallies, Bible studies, and a variety of other settings. Her book *I've Used All My Sick Days, Now I'll Have to Call in Dead* is a light-hearted, yet practical look at the stresses of daily life and has been featured on radio talk shows and highlighted on television interviews throughout the southeast. Cindi's "Frazzled Female Moment" can be heard daily on a variety of radio stations.

Cindi has also been involved in stress management training and related seminars for school systems, government agencies, state conferences, and corporate events.

Cindi earned a degree in intermediate education from Gardner Webb University in Boiling Springs, North Carolina. She has accumulated over 20 years of experience working with teachers, students, business leaders, and corporate administrators, helping them learn how to combat stress by managing time, developing a sense of humor, and learning to organize.

In recent years Cindi has felt the clear call to focus her experience and abilities on ministering to Christian women who, in spite of their faith, still feel overwhelmed, stressed out, frazzled, and in need of fresh hope and enthusiasm. Cindi's passion is to help women discover that a growing intimacy with Jesus Christ is the key to dealing with all areas of life—including the daily stress that often gets the best of us.

Cindi lives in Kings Mountain, North Carolina and is actively involved in ministry at First Baptist Church. She enjoys exploring life with best friend-husband, Larry. Sons Brandon and Lane keep her energized with life on the edge, while daughter-in-law Bonnie provides a calming influence.

To find out more about Cindi's ministry or to schedule a conference in your area, contact frazzledfemale.com or Regal Ventures Creative Ministries at 1-800-282-2561.

Welcome to the FRAZZLED FEMALE

Before you begin your study, let's look at some of the components. Four weeks of this study deal with things that distract us from, rather than attract us to, Jesus. The other two weeks explore our love relationship with the Lord. Each week has a memory verse. I encourage you to memorize it during the first day of study and meditate on it throughout the week.

Each week also includes a Defrazzler. This element will help you experience more deeply the concept you are studying that week. You may want to keep these strategies in place long after your study is complete.

The Weekend Mini-Retreat is an optional time of study. The retreat is designed to help you go deeper with the Lord as well as process what He has revealed to you throughout your week of study. This is a time for you to just be with Jesus, studying the Word and relaxing in His presence. The Book of John is the focus for these moments.

Don't feel guilty if you don't have time for a mini-retreat every week. You may need these times more some weeks than others. Be sensitive to the Lord's leadership when He leads you into this aspect of the study.

The daily sessions are designed to take 15 to 20 minutes, although you may spend much longer if you desire. The learning activities provide a time of reflection about how the study relates to you. You may be asked to express your feelings about things. These reflections may also be topics of discussion as you come together weekly with your small group to share what God revealed to you during your study. I strongly encourage you to complete all the learning activities to get the most from your study.

By participating in this study you are taking an important step toward sanity, peace, and spiritual growth. I am praying for you as you develop a deeper, more vibrant relationship with the Lord.

You'll need a pen, highlighter, and index cards to write your Scripture memory verses. Keep a notebook close to jot down thoughts the Holy Spirit reveals to you as you study.

Are you ready? The sooner you get going, the sooner you can become "victoriously frazzled"! God bless you in your study!

1 Mary Chose the One Thing Needed, So Will I!

❥ Memory Verse

"Seek first the kingdom of God and His righteousness, and all these things will be provided for you" (Matthew 6:33).

☢ Defrazzler

Create a rendezvous place for you and God! Design a special place so warm and inviting that you will want to go there, but not so relaxing you might fall asleep. Make sure you have adequate lighting, your workbook, a pen, a highlighter, and your Bible. You may also want to have index cards for Scripture writing and a prayer journal.

If you need some help choosing "your place," consider these suggestions:

- nook in the den or kitchen
- section of the closet
- porch or deck
- corner of the kitchen bar
- guest bedroom
- dining room table

Plan to meet God at this place every day as you go through this Bible study. It will become special to you as you store up memories and treasures in His kingdom!

☂ Weekend Mini-Retreat - John 1–4

Take time this weekend to "sit at the feet of Jesus." Use these chapters from the Book of John for your Scripture reading time with Him.

Think about the truths revealed to you this week. Praise Him. Love Him. Be still before Him. Enjoy Him. Allow Him to be to you all He wants to be!

Sometime during the weekend, journal about your experience.

Day 1 He Loves Me!

> 📷 **Focus**: Becoming intimate with God
>
> 🕮 **Scripture**: Begin by prayerfully reading Luke 10:38-42. Ask the Father to open your heart to hear His tender voice.

THE TRUE STORY

The movie was ending. Although Anna enjoyed the film, watching the syrupy love story on TV made her feel she was missing out on something in life.

Ed and Sally were caught up in a passionate romance. They had no children, jobs that left them with plenty of time to be together, and plenty of energy to take care of each other's needs. They spent hours talking and enjoying each other's company. Every part of their lives was absolutely wonderful because of the intimacy of their love.

I'll never experience that kind of love, was the thought that played over and over in Anna's mind.

Have you had an experience that left you feeling "love deprived"? ○ **yes** ○ **no   If yes, underline the words or phrases that describe how you felt.**

neglected	sad	empty
longing for something more	cheated	angry
helpless to make it happen	depressed	yearning for intimacy
lonely	needy	desperate
unfulfilled	unloved	other _____

The "true story" of every believer is the journey of the heart. The One who loves you most calls out to your heart every moment. Jesus longs for you to spend time in His presence, listening to His voice. In the middle of your daily stresses, He wants to have a relationship with you.

He wants you to step back from all the "good" things you are doing to experience the BEST thing: an intimate relationship with Him! He wants to say about you what He said about Mary, "Mary has chosen the One thing, the Best thing."

Many servants of the Lord work so hard for Him they bypass the one thing in life that's most important: an intimate love relationship with Jesus. Our Father does want us to minister to and meet the needs of others; however, our time with Him is more important to Him than anything we can "do" for Him. Out of this love relationship, ministry will naturally flow.

As a believer you have already chosen His gift of salvation, but have you chosen to accept what He has to offer you on a daily basis?

Check each statement which applies to you.

○ I have accepted Jesus Christ as my personal Savior.

○ I am experiencing an intimate relationship with Jesus on a daily basis.

○ I still feel unfulfilled in some areas of my life.

○ During much of my life I have not chosen to make intimacy with Jesus a priority.

○ I long for something to give my life deeper meaning.

○ Right now I am choosing to accept, by faith, the intimacy Jesus Christ invites me to experience.

If you have made the choice to begin this intimate relationship with your personal Lord and Savior, delight in the fact that the Father longs to experience a deep love with you. He has so much in store for you as you learn about His extraordinary love and seek to know His ways.

Pause now and offer this prayer of thanksgiving:

Dear Father, Thank You for desiring to have an intimate relationship with me. Bless my desire as I enter into this loving relationship with You and as I begin this study. I long to experience all the blessings that come with calling you Father. I love You and thank You for creating me and allowing me to be Your girl. Amen.

GETTING STARTED

One of the most exciting things about embarking on this journey of intimacy is that the Father will speak directly to you. One of the ways He does this is through Scripture. With this in mind, I encourage you to review the suggestions in the About the Study section on page 5. Apply them as you read the Bible passage at the beginning of each day's study.

I cannot describe the excitement that comes from realizing God is speaking to me and giving me a specific message as I read His Word. As I linger over a particular passage, He continues to reveal more of His Truth.

These revelations bring a new depth to Bible study. I used to just read the selected passage for the day in whatever devotional book I was using. Now my time spent reading God's Word is much slower and deeper. At times He leads me to focus on one or two verses during an entire day.

Opening your heart and mind to His voice as you read the words, phrases, and verses in the Bible is more important than what you read. Some days you will cover more material than others. We can learn to adjust to God's pace as He guides us daily during our time with Him.

Are you experiencing a deeper hunger, an excitement, and even a surge of joy as you think about getting to know Him better? Explain what you're feeling.

_____

_____

What you are experiencing is the pursuit of God. He is waiting and longing to fill your heart with unspeakable joy as you seek first His kingdom and righteousness!

What is God revealing to you today?

_____

_____

_____

As you close today's study, start your prayer time with this prayer:

Dear Father, I'm choosing You. I'm accepting the gift of Your intimate relationship. Thank You for pursuing me and longing to fill my life with Your intimacy. I love You.

Day 2 The Journey of Intimacy

> 📷 **Focus**: Understanding the nature of "sitting at His feet"
>
> 🔖 **Scripture**: Prayerfully review Luke 10:38-42. Make a note of words and phrases that speak to you in a personal way.

MARY AND MARTHA

Micki had heard about Mary and Martha for as long as she could remember. Pastors, teachers, and Christian speakers all pointed to Mary as the ultimate example of the devoted follower of God. Micki also recalled the picture her fourth grade Sunday School teacher painted of Martha being too busy to even notice Jesus, while Mary did nothing but sit and listen as He talked. Even as a child Micki remembered thinking, *How could anybody just sit and listen when there were so many things to do?* As an adult, she realized her feelings were much the same.

Have you ever felt that identifying with Mary is unrealistic for you? Explain.

_____

_____

SITTING AT HIS FEET

To have the proper view of Mary, we must understand the nature of "sitting at His feet." For me, it's being preoccupied with God. Each day I pull back from all other responsibilities and sit quietly with Him. Most of the time this is early in the morning when I begin my day. I read my Bible, sing softly to Him, talk to Him about what's in store for me that day, and pray for my needs and the needs of others.

Another way I "sit at His feet" is by simply thinking about Him throughout my day. I ask Him to go to the bank with me, help me as I get my groceries, be my companion as I drive across town, and give me the words I need before I make a telephone call. I invite Him to become involved in every detail of my life.

Reread Luke 10:38-42 and answer true (T) or false (F) to each statement.

___ Martha opened her home to Jesus.

___ Martha continued to enjoy His company before going about her duties.

___ Jesus pleaded with Martha to sit with Him.

___ Martha became distracted with everything that had to be done while Mary sat at the feet of Jesus.

___ Jesus rebuked Mary for not helping Martha.

Do you sometimes welcome Jesus into your "home," but then quickly go about your daily business, becoming distracted? Explain.

_____

_____

Our Heavenly Father longs for you to think about Him as you go about your daily activities. He wants to be part of every detail of your life—whether you're planning dinner or cleaning your desk at the office.

Which of these two ways of "sitting at the feet of Jesus" do you most often practice?

○ pulling aside from my daily activities to read my Bible and pray

○ thinking about God as I go through my day

○ both

Would you say you feel closer to Him during these times? Explain.

_____

_____

In the Amplified version of the Bible, we capture the full meaning behind the original Greek text. In verse 42 Jesus responds to Martha, "Mary has chosen the good portion [that which is to her advantage], which shall not be taken away from her."

An *advantage* is a favorable circumstance, a benefit. As we grow in intimacy with our Lord, we will notice many benefits. Following are some shared by women who are growing in their relationships with Jesus Christ.

"I am much calmer than usual."

"I'm laughing more and enjoying life."

"Things don't get to me like they used to."

"My children and I are getting along better."

"I'm not as short tempered as I used to be."

"My life seems to have more meaning."

"The more time I spend with Jesus, the more I grow to love Him." Of all the benefits mentioned, the last one seems to sum up this love relationship! I spend time with Jesus because I love Him. The more my love grows, the more I long to spend time with Him. Out of this love relationship, I experience many benefits (as do the people around me)!

What are some advantages you long to experience? Circle your answers.

a close friend	joy	peace	patience
a reason for living	excitement	feeling loved	hope
direction for my life	encouragement	self-control	other _____

Are you willing to explore a deeper love relationship with Jesus? If so, pause now and offer a prayer of commitment to your Heavenly Father, asking Him to grow your love for Him and your desire to be with Him.

List some things (errands to run, people to call, letters to write, meetings) that will make up your day. Circle the ones you will invite Jesus to be part of.

_____

What is God revealing to you today?

_____

_____

As you close today's study, start your prayer time with this prayer:

Dear Father, I yearn for the intimacy You have for me. I realize many of the things that take up my day are good things. I also realize I will never be fulfilled in any of them if I don't choose what's to my advantage, and that's sitting at Your feet! Help me get excited about being in Your presence. Help me long to listen to Your sweet whisperings that can only be heard when I spend time with You. I love You.

Day ❸ Hearing When God Speaks

> 📷 **Focus**: Experiencing God by thinking about Him during the day
>
> 🔖 **Scripture**: Read 1 Samuel 3:1-10. Ask the Father to open your mind to understand what He has for you in today's study.

INTIMACY IS A PROCESS

The beauty of the process is the joy we experience as we grow closer to the Lord. Unlike anything else in life, this quest for intimacy is divinely propelled. God loves for you to desire to grow close to Him, and He longs to delight your heart with His love! Consider Jesus' prayer to the Father as His crucifixion drew near. (See John 17:13 in the margin.)

Choose the statement that best summarizes intimacy with God.
- ○ Intimacy is a goal that can never be reached.
- ○ Growing intimate with God is a life-long process and one that is celebrated each step of the way.
- ○ It's easy to get discouraged trying to be intimate with God.

> "I am coming to You ... that My joy may be made full *and* complete *and* perfect in them [that they may experience My delight fulfilled in them, that My enjoyment may be perfected in their own souls, that they may have My gladness within them, filling their hearts]." *John 17:13,* **AMP**

In our relationship with Jesus, intimacy becomes a goal that is ever before us and is one that we can celebrate each step of the way.

Spend a few moments with the prayer of Jesus in John 17:6-9. Imagine the Father's joy when you come to Him, desiring to spend time with Him. Thank Him for pursuing this love relationship with you.

RECOGNIZING GOD'S VOICE

Samuel thought it was the priest, Eli, speaking to him. He was quick to respond when he heard his name called but did not recognize the voice of the Lord. Three times God called out to him. Each time Samuel rushed to the elder priest and answered, "Here I am." After that third time, Eli perceived that it was the Lord calling the boy.

In what ways has God spoken to you? Underline all that apply.

Scripture	through another person	in a song
prayer	nature	other _____

There may be times God is speaking to you throughout your day. Which of the following might keep you from hearing Him? Check all that apply.
○ I'm thinking about all I have to do.
○ My mind is preoccupied with negative thoughts of other people.
○ Financial worries are keeping me stressed.
○ My feelings are hurt about what someone said or did.
○ I'm not happy about the way I look or feel.
○ Other _____

It's natural to be preoccupied with life. Great demands are placed upon you in all the roles you play. You may be much like Samuel—simply preoccupied with your duties and not recognizing God's voice.

God keeps calling your name. He is so persistent with His love! He wants to enter into your busy schedule and minister to you and soothe you with His peace and His joy. Through spending time with Him and thinking about Him throughout your day, you will begin to recognize His voice.

Recognizing God's voice means experiencing Him. Experiencing God means being aware of His presence, His love, His joy, and His peace.

Someone may say something to you in conversation, and you know it is a word from God. Sometimes you may become acutely aware of beauty in nature, and hear God speaking. You may recall a Scripture passage during the day which speaks to a certain need, issue, or circumstance. These are all examples of God speaking to you!

Place a check by the statements that describe your experience.
○ I don't usually hear God speaking to me during a busy day.
○ When I think about Him during the day, I'm more likely to experience Him.
○ Spending time with God first thing in the morning, before my day begins, usually helps me focus on Him throughout the day.
○ The times I'm most at peace are the times I'm aware of His presence.
○ When I'm around others, I don't usually experience God's presence.
○ When I'm stressed out, I don't hear God speaking to me.

SPEAK, LORD. I'M LISTENING!

The fourth time the Lord spoke to Samuel, the boy responded, "Speak, for your servant is listening" (1 Samuel 3:10, NIV). This passage speaks to me of the consistency of God. He's unchanging in His love for us. Just as he continued to call Samuel, He continues to speak to us and pursue us wherever we are and whatever we are doing.

I can imagine the joy and excitement of young Samuel when he realized the Lord was speaking. He finally recognized God's voice and responded.

Excitement and joy are always present when you "hook up" with God. You must make the choice to desire Him and to experience Him. Will the response of your heart be, "Speak to me, Father. I'm listening"?

Rank the statements 1,2,3 with 1 being what must take place first for you to become more intimate with God.

____ I accept that God desires an intimate love relationship with me.

____ As I spend more time with Him in Bible study, prayer, and thought, He will continue to fill me with His joy.

____ I choose to accept His invitation of drawing me closer to Him and begin to desire a deeper relationship.

What is God revealing to you today?

_____

_____

As you close today's study, start your prayer time with this prayer:

Dear Father, I long to be in Your presence. As I understand more about how to become intimate with You, I know I will experience more joy and peace. It's exciting to think about how You want to spend time with me. Draw me closer to You. I love You.

Day ✿ 4 ✿ My Heart's Longing

> 📷 **Focus:** Deepening my relationship with my Father by pouring my heart out to Him
>
> ✎ **Scripture:** Ask God to speak to your heart as you read 1 Samuel 1:1-17.

UNFULFILLED LONGINGS

Hannah experienced the heart-wrenching turbulence of a longing unfulfilled. In ancient Hebrew society, for a wife to have no children was a terrible trial. She not only felt lonely and unfulfilled as a woman, but she also carried the burden of feeling she had displeased God. Since children were viewed as gifts from God, Hannah experienced a deep sense of guilt as well as the reproach of others.

Perhaps you are experiencing or have experienced a longing so intense it totally consumes your every thought. Check the sentences which most accurately describe how you feel now or felt in the past.

○ I can't seem to think about anything else.
○ My life seems robbed of joy.
○ I've poured my heart out to God, and He doesn't seem to hear me.
○ I don't know what I will do if ...
○ Nothing else seems to matter to me except ...
○ I keep trying to read the Bible and pray, but I still feel unfulfilled.

Often grief and self-absorption can lead to physical and emotional manifestations. Underline any you've experienced.

loss of sleep	physical aches and pains	lack of energy
loss of joy	inability to concentrate	extreme weariness
restlessness	lack of desire	other _____

GOD KNOWS THE LONGING OF YOUR HEART

I have listened as many women have poured out their heartaches to our loving God. The longings are as varied as the women themselves. While some women long for children, others long for Christian husbands. Some yearn to serve God in ministry, others are preoccupied with desires for their children. Whatever the deep desire of your life at this time, be assured that God knows, He understands, and He longs to be the answer to your need. The words of Jesus recorded in John 10:10 belong to you! (See margin.)

> "I have come that they may have life and have it in abundance."
> John 10:10

If the longing of your heart was satisfied at this moment, which of the following would you experience? Circle all that apply.

joy	freedom from worry	fulfillment
calmness	emotional stability	peace purpose in living
energy	confidence	frustration feelings of
usefulness	other _____	

Do you believe you have a loving Father who knows your needs and wants you to experience these things? ○ yes ○ no Explain your response.

_____

_____

HANNAH'S BURDEN BROUGHT HER TO GOD

"In bitterness of soul Hannah wept much and prayed to the LORD" (1 Sam. 1:10, NIV). If you identify with Hannah in the intensity of her longing, then you most likely identify with her bitterness. Hannah may have felt that she had reason to feel bitter about life and even about God. Circumstances in life can lead us to bitterness and may even cause us to question God's love for us.

Such are the thoughts God wants us to bring to Him. He longs for us to pour out our sorrow, our bitterness, our heartbreak to Him, so He can comfort us and ultimately give us the desires of our hearts.

Pause now and pour your heart out to your Heavenly Father who loves you and desires to fill you with His love, His joy, and His peace. Don't be afraid to say everything that's in your heart. He already knows your struggles, but He wants you to lift your inner self to Him.

Instead of allowing her distress to get the best of her, Hannah took her sorrow to the Lord. Prayer is the only way to gain strength to overcome both your emotions and your circumstances.

WHAT GOD GIVES IN RETURN

When I continue to run to Him with my burden, my focus gradually shifts from my burden to my God. As I spend more time talking to Him about my deep desires, I begin to realize He is reaching into my soul and is saturating my inner being with a desire for Him. Sticking with God when my prayers seem unanswered is only possible with the Lord's help.

Romans 8:26 says that the "Spirit himself intercedes for us with groans that words cannot express" (NIV). Persistent praying is the realization, based on faith, that He sees my need and longs to help me. This kind of praying takes me deeper into intimacy with the Almighty Father. If we allow Him, God uses our longing as a divine tool to bring us deeper into a relationship with Him.

WHEN GOD HAS SOMETHING BETTER IN MIND

As you turn your desires over to God, you invite Him to bless you by giving you His answer to your particular need. If God denies your request, He has something better planned for your life. I have come to the place in my life of choosing to give my yearnings to the Lord, followed with the prayer, "But Father, if You have something better in mind, cancel my request." That kind of prayer can only come from an intimate relationship based on faith and the knowledge that God's will for my life is always best!

God always answers prayers. "I call on the LORD in my distress, and he answers me" (Psalm 120:1, NIV). His answer may not be your way or your timing, but He always answers. Are you willing to offer Him the longing of your heart, so He may bring you closer into His love and meet your deepest need? Are you willing to allow Him to give you what He knows is best for your life?

This process will not happen overnight but will gradually grow as you spend time with Him, pouring out your heart and trusting Him to give you His best.

What is God revealing to you today?

_____

_____

As you close today's study, start your prayer time with this prayer:

Dear Father, I long to experience Your deep love in my life. Help me turn my deepest longings over to You. Show me how to trust You to meet the needs of my heart. Thank You for always answering my prayers. And thank You for giving me Yourself. I love You.

Day 5 Something More

> 📷 **Focus**: Holding on to your faith even when you don't "feel" like it
>
> 📖 **Scripture**: Ask the Father to draw you into His intimate presence. As you think about His love, prayerfully read Colossians 2:1-7.

SOMETHING IS MISSING

Patt had been a Christian for many years. She loved the Lord and enjoyed being involved in church. That's why it surprised her to realize she was becoming dissatisfied with life. It wasn't anything she could put her finger on; she just didn't feel like spending time with God the way she used to; and she wasn't enjoying the time she did spend with Him. She was very busy doing good things—God's things. All of her free time was spent "doing" things that revolved around her love for the Lord. She wondered what was happening in her walk with God. Why did she feel so blah?

When you have experienced a vibrant relationship with Jesus Christ, it's easy to get discouraged when you don't "feel" that excitement and joy.

Have you ever experienced a time in your Christian walk when your relationship with the Lord was less than exciting? If so, look at the following list. Place a check by the things you think contributed to the distant feelings you have experienced along your spiritual journey.

○ unconfessed sin   ○ being too preoccupied with other things

○ problems with people   ○ not taking time to "sit still" in His presence

○ difficulty focusing on God   ○ other _____

○ God creating a dissatisfaction so that I would seek Him more

When I go through those times of spiritual dissatisfaction, I cry out with the words of the Psalmist: "Search me, O God, and know my heart; test me and know my anxious thoughts. See if there is any offensive way in me, and lead me in the way everlasting" (Psalm 139:23–24, NIV). Willful and unconfessed sin will certainly create a barrier between you and God.

Take a moment and pray the prayer from Psalm 139:23-24. If it's your desire to intimately walk with the Father, consider the possibility that some sin in your life may be robbing you of a closer walk with Christ. After you have prayed, check the statement that applies to you.

○ God has revealed an area of sin in my life. In confessing that sin to Him, I am also turning my back on this behavior or thought. I am now restored to His fellowship.

○ As far as I can tell, there are no unconfessed sins in my life. What I am experiencing will pass as I stay close to God, allowing Him to lead me into a deeper love relationship with Him.

In Colossians, Paul writes to struggling Christians. He encourages them to be strengthened and comforted, having their roots firmly planted in Jesus and overflowing with thanksgiving.

It requires faith to be joyful when you don't feel the joy. Life on earth is like that. Sometimes you just don't "feel" happy. But Paul encourages us to remember what we were taught and to continue to overflow with thanksgiving.

GOD CAUSES YOU TO BE THIRSTY

A void in your spiritual life may lead you to thirst after God. In one of the greatest invitations ever offered, Jesus stood up in the middle of the crowds in Jerusalem and said, "If anyone is thirsty, he should come to Me and drink!" (John 7:37).

If you think about it, the reason you first came to Jesus was because of your thirst for Him: your longing to experience His love and salvation. Throughout your Christian walk the Father will place within you the desire to grow closer and closer to Him.

Briefly describe a time you experienced this kind of thirst for Him.

_____

_____

Paul viewed intimacy with Christ as the supreme goal in life. His prayer for believers is that we would "be encouraged and joined together in love, so that they may have all the riches of assured understanding, and have the knowledge of God's mystery—Christ" (Col. 2:2).

Pause and ask the Father to cause you to thirst after Him. Ask Him to fill you with the longing to become more intimately acquainted with Him and His ways.

ATTRACTED TO JESUS

When we become busy with too many things—even good things—our focus moves from the Lord to whatever we are doing. We can also become distracted with emotions, people, and time. Next week we will explore how negative attitudes can shift our focus from our relationship with God to our feelings about ourselves and others.

Paul reminds us to have the roots of our being firmly and deeply planted in Him, fixed and founded in Him so that we are constantly thinking about Him and overflowing with thanksgiving. (See Col. 2:7.)

Do you believe it's possible to "constantly" think about Jesus?
○ **yes** ○ **no Explain your response.**

_____

As you continue your journey through this study, be aware of God's love for you, His determination to pursue you, and His longing to experience a deeply intimate relationship with you. Thank Him that He never gives up on drawing you closer into His love.

What is God revealing to you about growing more intimate with Him?

_____

_____

As you close today's study, start your prayer time with this prayer:

Dear Father, Thank You for desiring my love. It's incredible to know You want an intimate love relationship with me. Help me desire You more than I ever have before. I open my heart and my life to You. I love You.

2

A Less Than Positive Attitude

❤ Memory Verse

"Pleasant words are a honeycomb, sweet to the soul and healing to the bones" (Proverbs 16:24, NIV).

☢ Defrazzler

This week you are going to fast! Before you imagine a growling stomach and a hearty appetite, let me say that it's a fast for the soul! I want to challenge you to take a 24-hour fast from a negative attitude. Think about an attitude that is robbing your joy and interrupting your thoughts. It may be a particular worry about a person or a situation. It may be critical thinking or a gloomy outlook.

When you push the attitude out of your mind, replace it with this week's memory verse. Say it aloud, sing it, shout it. Do anything necessary to keep negative thoughts at bay.

You have a helper in the Holy Spirit. He will guide you and give you the persistence you need in this endeavor. Ask Him.

☂ Weekend Mini-Retreat - John 5–8

Take time to sit at the feet of Jesus. Focus on being with Him, basking in His presence. As you read these passages, imagine Jesus' life on earth and how He interacted with those around Him. Pretend you're an eyewitness to His miracles. What is He wanting you to experience as you take a look at His earthly life and ministry?

Take some time during the weekend to record your reflections.

Day 1 A Positive Beginning

> 📷 **Focus**: Listening to God will help you be positive.
>
> 📖 **Scripture**: Begin today's study by giving this time to the Lord. Ask Him to speak to your heart as you read Genesis 12:1-9.

When God told Abraham to set out for a new land, Abraham chose to listen. He also chose to be positive about God's direction for his life. Abraham's obedience in his attitude and in his behavior caused him to be uprooted from his familiar way of life yet led him to discover God's greatness. He chose to trust even when God's promises seemed impossible to believe. Abraham sometimes strayed from the path by trying to work things out his way, but he continued to listen and be obedient as God called for his trust.

YOU HAVE A CHOICE

God called Abraham to leave his home and family and go to a foreign country. Abraham must have experienced some intense emotions!

Place a check by the statements describing how Abraham may have felt.
- ○ He was pleased God asked him to do such an exciting thing.
- ○ Leaving most of his family behind made him extremely sad.
- ○ Doubts filled his mind as he wondered if he had heard God correctly.
- ○ He was afraid and felt very insecure.
- ○ He was afraid of what people might think if he did such a crazy thing.
- ○ Although he didn't understand God's plan, he chose to trust Him.

Think of a time God asked you to do something difficult or risky. Underline the words or phrases that describe how you felt.

afraid	worried about the outcome
doubtful	wondering why God asked me to do such a thing
impatient	preoccupied with what others might think
hesitant	wanting to be obedient but feeling inadequate
anxious	other _____

Probably nothing in God's plan made sense to Abraham in the beginning. Perhaps that's how you felt when God asked you to step out of your comfort zone. However, in going with God Abraham headed in a positive direction. Anytime you listen to God and obey His words you are moving in a positive direction.

ABRAHAM MADE POSITIVE CHOICES

"[He] went, as the LORD had told him" (Gen. 12:4). Being obedient to the Lord is a sure way to move in a positive direction. Like Abraham's experience, your obedience might involve some difficult "moves" on your part. But any discomfort you experience will eventually lead you to God's blessings.

Describe a time you felt God was telling you to do something difficult, but you did it out of obedience to Him. How did God bless your obedience?

_____

_____

"I know the plans I have for you," declares the LORD, "plans to prosper you and not to harm you, plans to give you hope and a future." Jeremiah 29:11, **NIV**

As Abraham continued his journey of obedience, the Lord continued to reveal Himself and His plan. Abraham, in turn, worshipped God. "[Abraham] built an altar there to the LORD" (Gen. 12:7).

As you grow in your walk with the Lord and gradually develop a lifestyle of listening to Him and obeying Him, remember to worship Him along the way. Worship is an integral part of developing a positive lifestyle. We can rejoice in the truth of Jeremiah 29:11!

Pause and worship your Heavenly Father. Thank Him for taking care of you and giving you a future with Him.

Seeking God's direction in every part of life will help us become and remain positive. The more time we spend with Him, the more positive we will become!

**In which of the following areas do you need God's direction to become
more positive? Check all that apply.**

○ attitude   ○ behavior   ○ housework

○ relationship with: __ husband __ children __ friend __ coworker

○ other _____

Being positive involves more than what we think about. For the Christian
a positive attitude encompasses our whole being. We become positive by
listening to God, obediently following His directions, continually worship-
ping Him, and seeking His guidance.

What is God revealing to you about becoming a more positive person?

_____

_____

As you close today's study, start your prayer time with this prayer:

*Dear Father, I want to be more positive. Please make me aware of those
times when I say things and act in ways that are not pleasing to You. Teach
me to express myself in ways that truly bring You glory. Cleanse me from
negative thinking and infuse me with Your joy. I love You.*

Day 2 You Become What You Think

> 📷 **Focus**: Dwelling on positive thoughts will help you become
> positive.
>
> 🗝 **Scripture**: Spend a few minutes with the Father, asking Him
> to bless your time today. Attentively read Philippians 4:4-9.

Yesterday we focused on moving in a positive direction by listening to and
obeying God. Hopefully you have identified areas in your life where you could
be more positive. Do you see any of these areas in the list on page 26?
If so, place a check by them.

I need to be a more positive:

○ wife _____

○ mother _____

○ daughter _____

○ coworker _____

○ friend _____

○ other _____

Write the negative attitude(s) you need to get rid of in the blank beside each role you checked. If you need more room, make additional notes in the margin.

Your Defrazzler this week will help you become more positive. Have you chosen your "fasting attitude"? If not, do so now and complete the following.

I've chosen to take a fast on _____

Why? _____

How will your life be better by taking this fast? _____

_____

Finally brothers, whatever is true, whatever is honorable, whatever is just, whatever is pure, whatever is lovely, whatever is commendable—if there is any moral excellence and if there is any praise—dwell on these things.

Philippians 4:8

REPLACE THE NEGATIVE WITH A POSITIVE

When we toss out that negative attitude we have to put something in its place. With what should we replace it? We find the answer in Philippians 4:8.

When we spend time meditating on the Word, we are taking hold of the supernatural power of God. The benefits we gain by sitting at the feet of Jesus and spending time in His written Word are totally indescribable! So don't rush through your devotional time.

Reflect on the words of Philippians 4:8. Underline the phrases listed below that ought to fill our minds.

a godly relationship	Scripture	your dirty house
beauty found in nature	your lack of faith	praise
a broken relationship	how rotten you feel	celebration
a special time spent with God	Christian music	your blessings
a dream God has given to you	your inadequacy	a past sin

IT STARTS IN THE MIND

Are you beginning to understand how important it is to think positively? If you dwell on negative things, you will spout negative words and have negative facial expressions and body gestures. You can't *think* negatively and expect to *act* positively

Let's explore this concept a little further. To become the positive person God wants you to be you must first examine your negative thinking. Polling the general frazzled female audience of extremely busy women, I've collected a sampling of negative thoughts.

Place a check by any of these thoughts with which you identify.
- ○ I can't stand going home to a messy house after I work hard all day.
- ○ Thinking about cooking tonight makes me irritable.
- ○ If only my husband would help out with the kids.
- ○ Washing, cleaning, cooking, organizing ... I never get any thanks.
- ○ This job stinks. I wish I could do something I like.
- ○ Life is just one BIG chore after another.
- ○ My children don't do a thing to help around the house.
- ○ I'm tired of everybody else having a good time while I have to work around the house after working all day away from home.
- ○ There's never enough time for me.
- ○ All they do is talk. Why don't they get to work?
- ○ If she weren't such a busy-body she'd get more done.
- ○ My husband never pays attention to me.
- ○ Other _____

All of these may be reality for you. You may feel that many situations in your life have "created" your bad attitude. Before feeling justified in your negative thinking, take a look at what Paul (who was in prison at the time of this writing) says in divinely-breathed Scripture.

> "Rejoice in the Lord always. I will say it again: Rejoice!"
>
> Philippians 4:4

Place an R by each item on the negative thoughts list in which Philippians 4:4 tells us to rejoice.

If you placed R beside each statement, then you have the idea. According to Scripture, it's not a suggestion but a command to rejoice in the midst of all things. It won't happen overnight, but with determination you will gradually become more positive. With that movement of obedience comes God's grace, His blessing, and a positive attitude!

We'll continue to explore positive attitude building strategies this week. As we close today's study look back at verse 8 and the notes you took as you reviewed that verse. To help you practice dwelling on these things write:

a pure thought: _____

a lovely thought: _____

a praiseworthy thought: _____

As you close today's study, start your prayer time with this prayer:

Dear Father, I want Your thoughts to become my thoughts. I want Your words to become my words. Help me dwell on Your thoughts today, no matter what comes my way. I love You.

Day 3 The Power of God

Focus: Focusing on God's power in your life will help you "grow" a positive attitude.

Scripture: Talk to the Father right now, giving Him your love and adoration. Ask Him to speak to you directly as you read Ephesians 1. Seek to hear Him as you enter into today's study.

STRESS AND YOUR ATTITUDE

All week Debbie had been looking forward to sleeping in on Saturday. Every day she had gotten up at her usual "abnormally early" time just to get things done. Her week was filled with putting out fires—everybody else's. People were always wanting her to do something but were never satisfied with anything she did. Every time she made a little progress with her work, she had to add another item to her to-do list.

Early in the week Debbie promised God she would really try to have a more positive attitude. She told Him she wanted to spend more time with Him to soak in His goodness and joy.

However, she had an aging parent who took much of her time and a family that didn't help with housework. By the end of the week she was exhausted and grumpy. The only thing she looked forward to was sleeping late on Saturday morning.

On Friday night, Erin, Debbie's friend, called telling her that her husband, Jeff, had to report to work at 7 a.m. the following day. Erin was sick and wondered if Debbie could keep two-year-old Carly on Saturday. Jeff could drop her off on his way to work.

Imagine that YOU are Debbie. How would you feel about Erin's call?

_____

If you listed guilt or self-condemnation among your emotions, you are not alone. We often feel guilty over our initial reaction to stress. Describe a recent situation when you were overloaded with stress and reacted negatively.

_____

_____

Place an x by the statements that describe how you felt about your attitude.

____ I hate it when I say stupid things.
____ Once again, I've failed you Lord.
____ My witness is ruined.
____ I'm never going to get any better.
____ As soon as I get a little better, I mess up again.
____ Other _____

Life can be frustrating. It's often a real challenge to be positive when stressors are continually thrown your way. I have found that many times women can handle the big things in life that produce stress. Perhaps they have planned in advance for them and realize they are coming. However, the accumulation of common daily hassles often sneak up on them and rob their joy and positive attitude.

Look back at Debbie's story. Underline the events that could contribute to a negative attitude. How do you think these events affected her attitude?

_____

What things are accumulating in your life that negatively affect your attitude?

_____

GOD'S POWER IS AVAILABLE

Debbie talked to God about her attitude. Aware that she needed to improve in this area, she promised Him to do so. She also longed to spend more time with Him and planned to make this happen. Her plan, however, rested in her own strength, resulting in major frustration!

Have you ever told God you wanted to "do better"? ○ yes ○ no

Did you have difficulty with your "do better" plan? ○ yes ○ no

Why do you think people often have difficulty "doing better"?

_____

He demonstrated this power in the Messiah by raising Him from the dead and seating Him at His right hand in the heavens.
Ephesians 1:20

Even believers tend to forget it is the power of Jesus Christ living within us that enables us to become more Christlike. In Ephesians Paul prayed for those struggling Christians to realize the hope they have in Jesus.

Read Ephesians 1:20 in the margin and fill in the blanks.

The power available to me is the same power God exerted in the

_____ by _____ Him from the _____!

Check the areas where you've actually considered God's power being available to you.
- ○ cooking for my family
- ○ answering a phone call
- ○ grocery shopping
- ○ preparing for the holidays
- ○ driving on a trip
- ○ waiting in line
- ○ teaching a class
- ○ helping a friend
- ○ mopping the floor
- ○ singing a song
- ○ exercising
- ○ other _____

List three areas (be creative) where you have NEVER thought of God's power being available.

_____

Do you think God wants you to grasp His power in the areas you just listed?
○ **yes** ○ **no**

Read Ephesians 1:20 again. This same power is available to us to deal with other people, situations, and ourselves!

GRASPING THIS POWER

Spend the remainder of today's study time relaxing in the Lord. Meditate on the verses in Ephesians 1, focusing on this mighty power that is already yours as the daughter of your Father. Think of areas in your life where you want to begin to exercise God's power so your attitude may become more like the attitude of Christ. After you've had time to consider what the Father is revealing to you, make some notes about it in your journal or on a separate sheet of paper. You may want to think about this mighty power throughout the day and record your findings later.

As you close today's study, start your prayer time with this prayer:

Dear Father, In my efforts to have a positive attitude, I fail miserably. Help me to love myself even when I feel guilty for not being more like You. Remind me that Your power is available to me to do all the things that often trigger a rotten attitude. I long to be more like You. Cleanse me and empower me with Your love. I love You.

Day ✿ The Gift of His Power

> 📷 **Focus**: Exercising the power given to us by God to live a life that brings Him glory
>
> ◣ **Scripture**: Read Ephesians 2:1-10. Ask the Father to open your eyes to the reality of His power.

GOD'S POWER IN MY ATTITUDE

Yesterday we began to explore the availability of God's power. We learned that as His children we have the gift of accessing His power in every situation we face, including our daily attitudes! The power available to you to have a positive attitude is the same power God used when He raised Christ from the dead. How powerful is that?! What's your part in accessing this power? According to Ephesians 1:19, it is to believe.

I need to believe God for a positive attitude in ... Check all that apply to you.

○ relationship with my husband   ○ cleaning my house
○ relationship with my children   ○ helping with homework
○ time I spend at work   ○ doing yard work
○ trouble in a friendship   ○ being a caregiver
○ errands I have to run   ○ other _____

It's not difficult to find negative things to think and complain about. We live in a much less than perfect world. In fact, it's more natural to behave in a negative way than in a positive one. The challenge comes in *choosing* to be positive in a negative world. Only God can provide that positive attitude when daily living is so filled with stress.

SO, LORD, HOW DO I DO THIS?

At times I intellectually grasp a concept but I can't quite "plug it in" to my way of doing things. I find it so frustrating to understand what God is saying and yet remain uncertain as to how to put it to work in my life. When I get in one of these situations, I ask the Lord, "How do I do this?"

Write two "How do I do this?" questions to the Lord.

1. _____

2. _____

He will always answer when you call out to Him. As you seek Him and long to hear from Him, remember to be still long enough to experience His answer. Following are some of my experiences you may find helpful.

THE WORRY BOX

Anxiety and worry can lead to an extremely negative attitude. Ephesians 2 tells us this kind of thinking gratifies the craving of our sinful nature. Negativity keeps us busy with "self" obsessions. The enemy uses these as distractions to keep us from experiencing the peace of God which leads to a positive attitude and a life that glorifies God. Ephesians also states that because of God's great love for us, we have been made alive in Christ. And this new life of ours is a gift from God!

Years ago, I was impressed to give a gift back to the Father. I thought of worries that were occupying my mind, producing a cynical and negative attitude, and robbing me of my joy. I wrote them on separate sheets of paper and placed them in a box, giving them to the Father for a whole week. I committed to not think of these issues for a week.

Give it a try. Find a box (or any container) to put your worries in. Write them on slips of paper and place them in the box.

Place a check by the sentence when you have completed your task.
○ I have placed my worries in the worry box.

How does giving these worries to the Lord makes you feel?

_____

SCRIPTURE CARDS

I try to have a Scripture card handy while I'm waiting in line or anticipating a negative encounter (such as a confrontation or difficult conversation). This keeps me from allowing negative thinking to creep in. Instead of focusing on a negative thought, I pull the card out and focus on the Scripture.

Share a situation from the last couple of days when focusing on a Scripture could have helped you avoid negative thinking.

_____

_____

FOCUSING ON PRAISE

> And whatever you do, in word or in deed, do everything in the name of the Lord Jesus, giving thanks to God the Father through Him.
>
> Colossians 3:17

When I'm involved in a task that causes me to be irritated, "praise focus" becomes a delightful challenge. I often paraphrase Colossians 3:17: "Lord! I'm tired of cleaning up this kitchen, but I'm doing this for You and in Your name. I praise You for my family who made this mess at mealtime and for a physical body that can still clean."

You can be really creative with this one. And as you focus on the Lord and Scripture instead of the "event," you are empowered to glorify Him in everything you do.

You try. Think of a recent scenario where you could have practiced a "praise focus." Write your paraphrase of Colossians 3:17 below.

_____

_____

What is God revealing to you during your time with Him today?

_____

_____

As you close today's study, start your prayer time with this prayer:

Dear Father, Thank You for the gift of Your power in my life. Help me think of Your power often as I go about my daily activities. I love You.

Day ✿5 Being Positive in Negative Circumstances

> 📷 **Focus**: Being positive in the face of negative situations
>
> 🔖 **Scripture**: Ask the Father to reveal His purposes and ways to you as you prayerfully read Romans 4:18-25.

No way! Glenda thought as she read her devotional about being positive in the midst of trials. Through a simple story, the author challenged her at the very point of her vulnerability.

She had been engaged a year ago to a man she desperately loved and longed to spend her life with. Three weeks before the wedding, he walked away pledging his love to another.

Check three feelings you imagine were at the top of Glenda's emotional heap.
○ anger   ○ confusion   ○ embarrassment   ○ loss of self-esteem
○ betrayal   ○ shock   ○ rejection   ○ glad to be rid of him

Have you ever experienced these feelings or similar ones? ○ yes ○ no
Did you have a difficult time being positive? ○ yes ○ no   **Explain.**

_____

GOD UNDERSTANDS

As I was writing this study, I received a call from a friend who was experiencing difficulty with the concept of being positive when her world was falling apart. "It doesn't seem humanly possible," she said, "to be positive when so many bad things are happening to me. It doesn't seem realistic."

God understands our inability and even our resistance to being positive when everything inside us feels negative. He knows that in our weakness we are not able to overlook all of life's negatives and immediately jump into a positive lifestyle. He doesn't want us to ignore the facts of the negative situation, but He does want us to rely on His power to get us through one step at a time.

ABRAHAM WAS HOPEFUL

Based on your understanding of Romans 4:18-25, answer true (T) or false (F) to the following statements.

____ Abraham believed God because everything He said made sense.
____ Abraham knew God would do what He said He would do even though he had reason not to believe.
____ Abraham faced the fact that his body was as good as dead.
____ Abraham's negative outlook got the best of him, and God did not receive glory.
____ God continued to bless Abraham for his hope and positive attitude.

WE HAVE A REASON TO BE POSITIVE

As a Christian you have a reason to be positive! At times God may ask you to be positive and hopeful about a situation simply because He is God and He is in charge of your life.

The world says, "seeing is believing." The Bible says that we must "trust in, adhere to, and rely on God" (Romans 4:24, AMP). God wants you to believe Him first, without knowing the outcome of your situation!

Pause and ask the Father to touch your heart about a particular situation where you need His power to be more positive. It may be one you've already thought of during this week's study. Submit your free will to Him, asking Him to help you take small, positive steps of obedience.

Have you ever heard someone say, "I'm not being negative, I'm just being realistic"? Some people think being positive is not being realistic. That line of thinking is contrary to Scripture. Just like Abraham you can face each situation by choosing to place your faith and hope in God. As you practice this, you will develop a mind that is open to the will of God—whatever that may be.

Consider Glenda whose fiancé ran out on her. By adopting a negative attitude, Glenda might say, "My life is over. No one will ever want me again. I'm going to be miserable the rest of my life."

By being positive and realistic, Glenda could say, "I hate that this happened and I hurt so much. I know it's going to take time to get through this, but I trust God to restore me. He may send someone else my way if that's His will for me. God knows what's best for my life."

Day after day messages are being encoded in our minds. We carry on conversations with ourselves, interpret situations, and cast judgements. This self-talk can either be explosive and filled with doubt and criticism or positive and filled with hope. Here are some examples of self-talk.

"Why don't I just give up?"

"God is in control. Things are going to work out."

"I don't understand, but I trust Him."

"God must really be disappointed in me."

"I'm never going to make it through this."

"Father, I turn this over to You. I choose to believe You will take care of it."

Which of these examples do you most identify with right now?

_____

Is it positive or negative? ○ positive ○ negative

OUR PART IS TO BELIEVE

Sometimes, as hard as we try, we just can't make things happen the way we want them to happen. I believe God sometimes wants us to mentally, emotionally, even physically back off from a situation, allowing Him to reveal His glory as He resolves the issue. Romans 4 tells us that Abraham was strengthened and credited with righteousness as he believed God.

Do you need to back off a situation in your life right now, believing that God will resolve it and reveal His glory? ○ yes ○ no **If yes, commit to giving this to God.**

What is the Lord revealing to you right now?

_____

_____

As you close today's study, start your prayer time with this prayer:

_Dear Father, You are speaking to me through Your love about the negatives in my life. Thank You for understanding my weakness, my hurt, my frustration. I place _____ in Your keeping right now. I believe You love me and You will take care of this situation. Reveal Your glory. I love You._

3

I Don't Have Enough Time!

👄 Memory Verse

"Your heart must not be troubled. Believe in God; believe also in Me" (John 14:1).

☢ Defrazzler

This week you are going to create a detail book. Find a small notebook in which you can jot down your to-do list each day. List things you really need or want to do before day's end: stop by the grocery, pick up dry cleaning, call a neighbor who is sick, make an appointment.

I take a few moments in the morning or the evening before to make my list and pray over each item. My day goes more smoothly when I lift these items to the Father before I do them. Praying over your to-do list is a way of offering your entire day— even the little things— to Him.

In the front of my detail book I wrote: *Lord, here's my list of details. I'm recording things to do, errands to run, items to pick up, places to be, calls to make … all the things that can drive me crazy if each one is not committed to You! Thank You for being the Lord of my details!*

☂ Weekend Mini-Retreat - John 9–12

Consider Jesus' life as painted in these Scriptures. Hear His authority as He heals the blind man. Capture His tenderness as He weeps with Mary and Martha over the death of Lazarus. Imagine the aroma of the perfume as Mary lovingly bathed her Savior's feet. Is your mind capturing the love of Jesus like never before?

Sometime during the weekend, journal about your experience.

Day 1 God Is in Control

> 📷 **Focus**: Focusing on God instead of circumstances
>
> 📖 **Scripture**: Prayerfully read Exodus 2:1-10. Open your heart to your Father, asking Him to bless this time.

JOCHEBED AND HER CIRCUMSTANCES

God had given Jochebed, the mother of Moses (Exodus 6:20, NIV), the gift of a beautiful baby boy, yet Pharaoh had ordered the death of every Hebrew male baby. How overwhelming her circumstances must have seemed!

The mother of Moses knew God. Knowing Him led her to trust Him to take care of her child. Hebrews 11:23 tells us she disobeyed the king by hiding Moses for three months. What a courageous act of faith to place her baby in the bulrushes at the river's edge.

As a woman who loved God and understood the yearning of her own heart, Jochebed trusted Him completely with the welfare of her child. Her faith was rewarded as God inclined the heart of the Pharaoh's daughter to save the child, making his mother his nursemaid.

Underline what you think may have been three of Jochebed's most intense emotions as she lowered Moses into the basket.

anger	expectancy	hopelessness	gratefulness
loneliness	hopefulness	distress	weariness
fearfulness	desperation	anxiety	determination
peacefulness	excitement	helplessness	victimization
faithfulness	guilt	worry	inadequacy

Give a reason for each emotion you chose.

1. _____

2. _____

3. _____

LIFE CAN BE UNSETTLING

Jochebed was in the middle of an unsettling circumstance yet she trusted that God was in control. You no doubt have experienced unsettling circumstances as well.

In my seminars I ask the question, "What causes you to be frazzled?" "Not enough time" is always at the top of the list.

Mark an X on the continuum indicating how much time you have for each area of your life. Skip the statements that don't apply to your current life situation. 0 = not enough time; 5 = adequate time; 10 = too much time

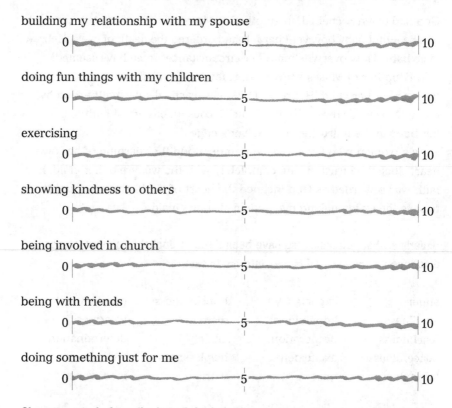

building my relationship with my spouse

0 —————————5————————— 10

doing fun things with my children

0 —————————5————————— 10

exercising

0 —————————5————————— 10

showing kindness to others

0 —————————5————————— 10

being involved in church

0 —————————5————————— 10

being with friends

0 —————————5————————— 10

doing something just for me

0 —————————5————————— 10

Choosing words from the list of Jochebed's emotions, list some of your own feelings about the unsettling circumstance of TIME.

_____

_____

MEETING LIFE'S CHALLENGES

I'm sure Jochebed drew from her maternal instincts in designing a plan she hoped would protect her baby. More importantly, she drew strength from her God who led her through a mission to protect and preserve not only the life of her young child but an entire nation of God's children. How the Hebrew people would be blessed through the faithful leadership of Moses!

Through Jochebed's example we can learn two important principles of time management. First, Jochebed relied on God. Secondly, Jochebed was persistent. Her firm faith gave her the strength she needed to do what God called her to do.

Place a check by the items on the last activity with a score less than 5. How many did you check? _____ Pause right now to pray. Ask the Father if He wants you to give more time to these areas of your life. Seek His counsel about how to spend more time in each area.

It takes tremendous faith, discipline, and persistence to manage your time God's way. As we work on time management principles this week, be open to God's guidance. Perhaps it's time for you to seek His counsel about what you do with the time He has given you. Just as He did for Jochebed, He will reward you with His strength, joy, and provision.

What is God revealing to you about how you are managing your time?

_____

_____

As you close today's study, start your prayer time with this prayer:

Dear Father, I often feel overwhelmed with all I have to do. There never seems to be enough time to get everything done! Right now I'm seeking Your guidance. Please show me how to make the most of my time so I may bring glory to You. I love You.

Day 2 More...

> 📷 **Focus**: Making time with Jesus a priority will lessen the pressure of time issues.
>
> 🗝 **Scripture**: Let the reading of Matthew 6:19-34 draw your focus to Jesus and His intense love for you. Worship Him as you read.

NEVER ENOUGH TIME

Betty read in the Sunday church bulletin that a ladies' Bible study would begin next week. Her heart jumped with excitement as she anticipated gathering with Christian women to study and talk about Scripture. She longed to grow in her relationship with the Lord. She wanted to experience His peace and joy in her life on a daily basis.

By Thursday night, Betty was exhausted from working at her daily job and coming home to begin "second shift": the title she gave her responsibilities at home. Once again, she shelved the idea of the Bible study, feeling she didn't have enough time. She would attend when life wasn't so busy.

Write YES in the blanks beside the phrases you identify with in Betty's story.

_____ longing to grow in relationship with the Lord
_____ wanting to experience His peace and joy
_____ exhausted from working at daily job
_____ coming home to begin second shift
_____ not enough time for a Bible study
_____ will join a Bible study when life isn't so busy

Name something you put off because you were tired and busy.

_____

Did you go back and do it? ○ yes ○ no **How do you feel about your decision?**

_____

TREASURES IN HEAVEN

I pray as you go through this week's study you will be open to the Father's revelation concerning time issues. He alone can give you specific guidance to deal with the "time stress" in your life.

Pause and prepare your heart to receive His message for you through the Scriptures. Thank Him for caring about your time.

Consider these scenarios:

Sue's daughter, Heather, plays soccer. During soccer season Heather's afternoons are filled with soccer practice. After work Sue goes to watch practice. She and Heather usually grab a bite to eat on the way home.

Is this an example of storing up treasures in heaven? ○ yes ○ no Explain.

_____

_____

Liza shared this with our Bible study group: "When I walked into my kitchen at 6 a.m. I looked at the dirty dishes in the sink and then at my Bible. For a moment I was torn about what to do. Doing the dishes would give me a head start on my day, but I wouldn't have time for Bible study. I decided to read my Bible. I had the most wonderful experience with God. The rest of my day went smoothly because I was filled with His peace."

Is this an example of storing up treasures in heaven? ○ yes ○ no Explain.

_____

Have you ever had an experience similar to Liza's? What happened?

_____

HAVING MORE

Both of the above experiences could be examples of storing up treasures in heaven—depending on how you use your experiences to glorify God and what He wants you to do with your time.

I can't possibly know what's best for you in any area of your life, but your Father does. That's why it's so important to talk to Him about it. You will not have more time if you make Jesus a priority in your life, but the time you have will be MORE!

More is what Liza experienced when she made time with Jesus a priority over household chores. He gave her what she needed to complete each task. What a divine thing He does for us when we spend time with Him!

How often do you make time with Jesus a priority? Circle the number.

1　　　　2　　　　3　　　　4　　　　5

hardly ever　　　　sometimes　　　　every day

TURNING A MARTHA DAY INTO A MARY DAY

Jesus speaks directly to Martha in Luke 10:42, "Mary has made the right choice, and it will not be taken away from her." When we daily make a divine appointment with Him, we will experience tremendous blessings to deal with our daily activities. Satan will use the "I don't have time" attack to try to keep us from Bible study and prayer. But it's our responsibility to make sure nothing stands in the way of our time with Jesus—especially when we don't have time!

In what areas of your life do you specifically long to experience His blessings? Underline them.

as a mother　　　as a wife　　　at work
cleaning house　　　in my friendships　　　serving others
in my time with God　　　other _____

Do you believe spending time with Him each day will lead you to experience His blessings? ○ yes ○ no Explain.

_____

Circle three blessings you long for right now in your life.

peace　　　joy　　　patience
intimacy with Jesus　　　faithfulness　　　obedience
Christlike love　　　endurance　　　gentleness

This week's defrazzler will help you experience greater peace in your daily activities. Some women are tempted to make only a mental list. I encourage you to write the items down daily and pray over each one. One excited Bible study member exclaimed, "This is how you turn a Martha day into a Mary day!"

What are some truths He is revealing to you about time issues in your life?

_____

_____

As you close today's study, start your prayer time with this prayer:

Dear Father, I long for Your peace in all I do. Lord, I want to do what's to my advantage and to Your glory. Help me commit to sit at Your feet daily. Give me the persistence to do this, especially when I don't have time. I want to experience Your peace and joy in my life. I love You.

Day ❸ The Core of the Problem

> 📷 **Focus**: Determining the things God wants me to do right now
>
> 🔖 **Scripture**: Prayerfully read Isaiah 55, asking your Father to open the eyes of your heart so He may speak to you.

Emily managed to get away from her family to attend a women's retreat for the weekend. As she sat in a crowded auditorium with other women who shared the same frustrations of having too much to do and too little time, she heard these words: "God will not bless you in doing the things He has not called you to do." Emily was stunned. Her life was full of good things. Could it be God didn't want her to do *all* these things?

Do you, like Emily, have a life filled with doing good things? ○ yes ○ no

Check the "good things" that apply to you. Add others that are not listed.
○ teaching Sunday school   ○ mentoring   ○ volunteering
○ working outside home   ○ leading youth   ○ being a wife
○ serving on a committee   ○ joining clubs   ○ being a mother
○ being a friend   ○ singing in the choir   ○ tutoring
○ serving in a civic organization   ○ other_____

TOO MANY GOOD THINGS

I know many women who have filled their lives with too many good things! Many Christian women, swallowed up in an endless array of duties, responsibilities, and service, miss out on God's best for them. This plethora of activity often steals their creativity, their play-time, their joy, and leaves them physically, emotionally, mentally, and spiritually depleted.

To what degree are you depleted? Mark your response on the continuum.

not at all   somewhat   very

Check the areas where you are experiencing depletion.
○ Physically   ○ Emotionally   ○ Mentally   ○ Spiritually

Does depletion in any or all of these areas affect your relationships, including your relationship with God? ○ yes ○ no **Explain.**

_____

_____

GOD HAS AN INVITATION FOR YOU

Through Isaiah, God issues an invitation to all who are thirsty, to all who are not satisfied with life, to all who are too busy to enjoy His peace and joy. I assure you if you are anxious, pressured, and depleted by the demands placed on your life right now, God has something better in mind for you. Too little time is not actually the problem. The core of the problem may be having too much to do!

God does not want you to do every good thing. I can't tell you what you should do, but He can. That's why you must check His thinking and seek His counsel in everything you do. Isaiah 55:6,8 admonishes us to seek the Lord and consider His thoughts and ways. He alone can tell you what you need to be involved in during this time in your life.

SEEKING THE LORD

List your roles in each of the following areas. Skip those that don't apply.
(Example: Family: wife, mother, chef, housekeeper, soccer mom)

Family: _____

Church: _____

Career: _____

Community: _____

Schools: _____

Friendships: _____

Volunteer work: _____

Other: _____

Reread your list and place a check by the areas where you may be overcommitted. Take time with the Lord, seeking His direction. Remember, sitting at His feet and seeking His counsel are to your advantage!

After your prayer time, share what the Father is revealing to you. Are there areas He wants you to give up? Are you affirmed in your roles in other areas?

_____

_____

As you close today's study, start your prayer time with this prayer:

Dear Father, I now understand the importance of seeking Your counsel in every role in my life. Speak to me. Continue to show me Your plan for my life. I want Your peace.

Day 4 Blessed by God

> 📷 **Focus**: Finding beauty in the consistency of the relationship
>
> 🔖 **Scripture**: Read Proverbs 31:10-31. Ask God to fill you with spiritual excitement as you grow in the qualities of His ideal woman.

COMPARING MYSELF TO OTHERS

Sue's heart sank as she considered the description of the virtuous woman in Proverbs 31. She had recommitted her life to God, asking Him to show her how to be the woman He wanted her to be. She also asked Him to show her how to get everything done on a daily basis, glorifying Him in the process. She was flooded with feelings of guilt and self-doubt as she read through the qualities of God's ideal woman.

Have you ever compared yourself with a woman you perceived as "better" at doing things God's way? ○ yes ○ no **If yes, how did that make you feel?**

_____

Place a check by the statements you felt verified her superiority to you.
○ She's always in a good mood.
○ Her children are well behaved.
○ Her house is always clean.
○ She is organized.
○ She gets so many things done.
○ Everybody likes her.
○ She is close to God.
○ She's the perfect wife.
○ She never gets upset.
○ Her clothes are always in style.
○ Other _____

Did God tell you to compare yourself to this woman? ○ yes ○ no **Explain.**

_____

At times God may give you an example in another person. He may speak to you through the words or lifestyle of that person, drawing you to His character. Other times you may initiate the comparison, and the focus becomes jealousy and self pity because you can't seem to "measure up."

God gives you the picture of a virtuous woman in Proverbs 31 because He longs for you to experience the glories of living such a life. He has a specific plan for you at this precise time in your life.

GOD'S IDEAL WOMAN

She was up before dawn.
She had her own garden.
She made clothes for herself and her family.
She owned and ran her own business.
She was a wonderful homemaker.
Her husband praised her.
Her children adored her.
She was intelligent.
She took care of the physical needs of her family.
She spoke with wisdom.
She helped others.
She was in shape—physically, mentally, emotionally, spiritually.
She feared God.

Draw a smiley face beside the characteristics you are pretty good at "pulling off." How many do you have left? _____

How do you see your potential to become the ideal woman? Check one.
◯ There's hope for me. I think I can become God's ideal woman.
◯ Maybe—with a lot of work—I can become God's ideal woman.
◯ Nope. I can't do it. I'll never be what God wants me to be.

You CAN become the ideal woman—not because of what you can do but because of who He is.

Look back at the characteristics describing this mega-woman. Knowing what Scripture says and knowing the focus of this Bible study, what do you see as the most worthy and admirable descriptive?

She _____ _____!

She feared God. According to The Amplified Bible, the virtuous woman worshipfully feared the Lord. She put God at the top of her priority list! Only one thing is mentioned in Proverbs 31:30 as making her value "far above rubies"—her spiritual life. It ALL goes back to sitting at the feet of Jesus!

As you worship Him, read His Word, and seek His counsel, God will tell you what things should be part of your life. Planting your garden may sow seeds of kindness through a volunteer project or might show particular interest in a family member's activities. Being a wonderful homemaker may offer daily encouragement to your husband, listen to your child pour out frustrations about friendships, or write encouraging notes.

You will be strengthened spiritually, mentally, emotionally, and physically as you make God-time your top priority.

Look at the following phrases taken from The Amplified Bible of Proverbs 31. Write M for mental, P for physical, E for emotional, and S for spiritual beside the statements you believe describe that characteristic.

____ "She rises while it is yet night and gets [spiritual] food."

____ "She considers a [new] field before she buys ... not courting neglect of her present duties by assuming other duties."

____ "She girds herself with strength ... physical fitness for her God-given task and makes her arms strong and firm."

____ "She looks well to how things go ... the bread of idleness, [gossip, discontent, and self-pity] she will not eat."

In which area—mental, physical, emotional, spiritual—do you most need strengthening? Explain.

_____

Be affirmed and encouraged, dear sister. God longs for you to experience peace in your daily activities. He wants your life to be filled with joy, not turmoil and panic. He invites you to the place of ultimate comfort, rest, fulfillment, and excitement: His presence.

What is the Father speaking to you as you come to the end of today's study?

_____

_____

As you close today's study, start your prayer time with this prayer:

*Dear Father, I know You have a specific plan for me on a daily basis.
I realize You will never make me place You as priority of my life. I ask
that You continue to draw me to You and give me joy and excitement
as I think about spending time with You. I love You.*

Day 5 My Time Belongs to God

> 📷 **Focus**: Managing my time is a big part of managing myself.
>
> 🔖 **Scripture**: Prayerfully read Psalm 27. Ask God to speak plainly to
> you, filling you with His hope and encouragement.

LIFE IS DIFFICULT AT TIMES

For three weeks Patti had gotten up early each morning to have time alone
with God. She felt good about the new direction in her life. Her stress level
and the way she handled herself during the day seemed different. But last
week her mother went into the hospital and everything changed. Patti
no longer experienced the depth of peace she had before the event. She
was racing around, daily spending time at the hospital and caring for her
family. What went wrong?

**Can you identify with Patti's feelings of doing things "right" and still experiencing
a lack of peace because so much is crowded into your day?** ○ yes ○ no

Describe a time in your life when you experienced similar frustrations.

_____

Many times circumstances seem to fire at us like an enemy attacking. During
some seasons, the daily pressures of getting things done will get you down.
Sometimes extra work and duties will be required because of unexpected
events, as well as the events for which you plan. During these times, you
may feel you need 48 hours in a day to accomplish all you need to do.

Have you ever felt like you needed twice the hours in a day to get things done? ○ yes ○ no If so, describe the circumstance.

_____

Circle the events that have caused you to feel especially pressured about time.

caring for a sick parent   planning a wedding
going back to school   renovating a house
raising children   hosting a party
starting a business   doing yard work
moving   changing careers
taking a trip   other _____

MANAGING SELF

If *time* seems out of control, it may be that *you* are out of control. Perhaps you can eliminate some of your time stressors. Seek the Lord's guidance in what needs to go. At times you do not have control of time factors, but you do have control of your reaction to circumstances. Take another look at Psalm 27:3–5.

What is the one thing the psalmist asks of the Lord? (v. 4)

_____

Who will keep you safe in the day of trouble? (v. 5)

_____

"Managing self" means to do what I can do with *me* when I can't do anything about the circumstances surrounding me.

As you have talked with the Father this week regarding the time issues in your life, did He tell you to let go of something? ○ yes ○ no If yes, what is it?
_____ Have you obeyed? ○ yes ○ no

Are there other areas you cannot let go of but need God's peace to get you through? Explain.

_____

SET ME HIGH UPON A ROCK

The description found in Psalm 27:5 truly speaks to me. At times I cry out to my Heavenly Father to "come get me" and set me high above my circumstances, bringing me close to Him!

The Father gave me a powerful visual to help me see He indeed is ALL I need as I travel through stressful times. Though I was pulled and stretched in many directions, I simply cried out to Him to restore my joy and peace—not to mention my sanity. In my journal I wrote *JESUS.* Around His name I wrote the names of events and people who were occupying my time. In doing so, I realized that the "things" that were occupying my time, mind, and energy (no matter how important) could easily steal my focus from Jesus.

When my focus shifts from Him, my energy is divided and my stress is multiplied. As long as He is central to my thinking and my commitment, I experience His peace and joy—no matter what else is going on in my life.

When you keep your focus on Jesus, He fills you with a peace and joy the world cannot give.

Place a check by the desires which describe your longings right now.
- ◯ I want Jesus to lift me above my circumstances.
- ◯ I want His peace and joy in all the things I'm doing.
- ◯ I want His energy to fill my body so I can accomplish all I must do.
- ◯ I want freedom from self condemnation.
- ◯ I want to enjoy life with Jesus, my family, and friends.

The Father will not turn His back on the longings of your heart. Love Him, trust Him, be strong, and take heart as you focus on Him. Pray Scripture to Him. Think about Him. Bask in His love.

What is the Father revealing to you today?

_____

_____

As you close today's study, start your prayer time with this prayer:

Dear Lord, Thank You for being the Lord of my time. Restore my joy, peace, and sanity. Give me insight and persistence to keep my focus on You. Fill me with assurance of Your love and Your desires for me. I love You.

4

People are Getting on My Nerves!

🐦 Memory Verse

"If possible, on your part, live at peace with everyone" (Romans 12:18).

☢ Defrazzler

This defrazzler will not only benefit you, but it will directly affect the life of another person. During your waiting times this week, focus on an individual: your waitress, a bank teller, a receptionist, or the person sitting in the next car. Ask the Father to direct you. He will draw you to a particular person. As you wait, pray specifically for that individual. The Holy Spirit will always impress upon you how to pray if you ask Him.

Anywhere you find yourself waiting, begin to pray. Your waiting time will take on new meaning. Write about some of your prayer moments in your journal.

☂ Weekend Mini-Retreat - John 13–16

Find some time during your busy weekend to relax with Jesus as He speaks to you through these chapters. Imagine Him washing your feet just as He washed the feet of His disciples. What is He saying to you?

Understand His comforting words, and accept the gift of the Holy Spirit to help you through your trials. Be refreshed in a new way as Jesus describes Himself as the true vine. Commit to abide in Him in a deeper way.

Take some time during the weekend to record your reflections.

Day ❀ Living Peacefully

> 📷 **Focus**: Finding peace with self leads to peace with others.
>
> 📚 **Scripture**: After reading John 14:1-27, ask the Father to help you identify areas where you feel insecure and troubled.

A few words spoken by another can throw you off track and disrupt your peace. Jesus' words had this effect on His disciples as He prepared them for His heavenly departure.

Identify a time when you experienced great pain from the words of another. Circle the words below that best describe how you felt.

shocked	judged	angry	sad
mistreated	condemned	undeserving	wounded
frightened	confused	overwhelmed	convicted
surprised	attacked	wronged	alone
hurt	betrayed	embarrassed	other_____

How do you think your feelings matched those the disciples experienced as Jesus explained His departure?

_____

WHAT ABOUT ME?

The disciples left everything to follow Jesus. Then Jesus told them He was going away. He was actually leaving them! Philip and Thomas spoke for the group in verses 5 and 8. They desperately wanted to understand Jesus, and they wanted an answer to the question: "What about me?"

Self lies at the heart of many problems we face in dealing with people. We want to know: *Why are you telling me this? What am I supposed to do? How should I feel? Who is going to help me? Why don't you understand me? Don't you care about me? What's going to happen to me?*

Think of a situation in your life when you asked similar "self" questions. What questions did you ask?

_____

_____

_____

Sharon works in an office with five other people. They often have lunch together and chat during breaks. Recently Sharon realized that Alesa is acting differently toward her. She seldom speaks and when she does it's with a condescending tone. Alesa's unfriendly attitude is beginning to bother Sharon. She wonders what happened to cause Alesa's actions.

Think of a time someone's attitude made you wonder why he or she was acting a certain way toward you. Check the questions you asked yourself.
○ Why am I being treated this way?
○ What did I say or do?
○ What did someone else say about me?
○ What can I do to make everything okay?
○ Other _____

JESUS OFFERS HIS PEACE TO YOU

"Peace I leave with you; My [own] peace I now give and bequeath to you. Not as the world gives do I give to you. Do not let your hearts be troubled, neither let them be afraid. [Stop allowing yourselves to be agitated and disturbed; and do not permit yourselves to be fearful and intimidated and cowardly and unsettled]" (John 14:27, AMP).

Circle the words in the above passage that describe how you felt in a recent unsettling situation involving another person.

Jesus said we don't have to be troubled, afraid, agitated, intimidated, or unsettled. He has given us His peace! Just like the disciples and Sharon, we sometimes let the words and behaviors of others cause us to feel confused. It's good for us to recognize our unsettled feelings, but it's not productive to get self-absorbed in the process.

When we move our focus from self to the peace that Jesus offers, we open the door to understanding by getting self out of the way. Take a look at John 14:16. Jesus told us we are not alone in achieving peace. He has sent a Comforter, Counselor, Helper, Strengthener, and Standby to remain with us in every situation we face.

Are you experiencing people difficulties? If so, write the initials of three people who come to mind.

1. _____ 2. _____ 3. _____

Focus on one of the people you just listed. To what degree are you troubled in that relationship? Circle the number.

1	2	3	4	5
not troubled				very troubled

We will continue to explore ways to achieve God's peace in our relationships. Lift the particular person you identified to the Father. Ask Him to lead you to a place of peace so you may be a witness for Him in this relationship. Rest assured that the Holy Spirit is by your side to give you all the help you need.

What is God revealing to you in today's study?

_____

_____

As you close today's study, start your prayer time with this prayer:

Dear Father, Thank You that Your peace is available to me. I know You love me. I know You love all Your children. I realize it's Your desire that I do my part to get along with _____. Be my helper as I give this relationship to You. I love You.

Day 2 Depends on Me

> 📷 **Focus**: Learning to do my part to get along with others
>
> 📖 **Scripture**: As you read Romans 12, ask the Father to show you how to live in harmony in your relationships.

The Book of Romans is a personal letter from Paul to the church in Rome. In chapter 12 Paul addresses the differences in people. We may have different spiritual gifts, different behavioral styles, and different ideas of right and wrong. But Paul encourages believers to aggressively reach out to others through Christ's love, regardless of differences.

DIFFERENCES CAN CAUSE CONFLICT

In my work with the Frazzled Female seminars, I have discovered that many women become frustrated because of differences in people. Perhaps you are experiencing similar frustrations.

Circle the words that represent people who frustrate you.

husband	children	coworker	boss
parent	sibling	customers	church people
neighbor	other drivers	telemarketers	friend
other _____			

Underline the words and phrases that describe those who frustrate you.

messy	too talkative	unorganized
don't care	indecisive	don't help around the house
too quiet	unappreciative	never want to talk about things
argumentative	bossy	take too long to get things done
too orderly	other _____	

In working with women I have found the woman often determines the attitude in the home. I'm not sure why that's the case, but I've noticed it often is. I realize that when everyone comes home after a busy day, my attitude sets the tone for the family's mealtime conversation.

Paul speaks directly to us in Romans 12:18. (See margin on page 59.) Our responsibility in any relationship is to live at peace. Let's explore this concept more deeply as we consider our personal role in getting along with others.

Write the names of three people with whom you are experiencing difficulty. (These may or may not be the same people you listed yesterday.)

1. _____

2. _____

3. _____

Within these relationships, how are you feeling? Check all that apply.

○ irritated   ○ unappreciated

○ misjudged   ○ like my feelings don't matter

○ angry   ○ like I'm responsible for everything

○ overlooked   ○ other_____

According to Romans 12:18, what is your part in getting along with these people? To _____ ____ _____ with them.

One of the ways to do that is to get self out of the way!

"If possible, on your part, live at peace with every-one." Romans 12:18

DOES IT HURT THE CAUSE OF JESUS, OR DOES IT HURT ME?

Dana works hard in her church. She works in the nursery, helps clean up after church suppers, sings in the choir, and facilitates women's Bible studies. Many women regularly attend the studies she leads because they learn a lot from Dana and enjoy the things she shares.

Recently another women's Bible study was offered at the same time as the one Dana is leading. Dana learns a week before the new study begins that most of the women who regularly sign up for her studies are enrolled in the new class.

If you were Dana, how might you feel? Write two sentences expressing your feelings.

1. _____

2. _____

The normal human reaction would probably be one of hurt. Maybe Dana wonders if she has offended the ladies who regularly attend her studies. She may be tempted to confront them about why they no longer want to be in her class.

Could the hurt Dana experiences (justified or not) possibly cause her to be self-absorbed? ○ **yes** ○ **no**

What about the relationships that are causing you hurt, frustration, anger, disappointment, fear, heartache? Are your feelings causing you to take your focus off Jesus by becoming self-absorbed?

These self-feelings are normal. They are part of being human. But to live at peace with everyone, we must stop focusing on ourselves and start focusing on Jesus.

When I suffer pain in a relationship, I am learning to ask the question, "Is the cause of Jesus being hurt or are my feelings being hurt?" When I am preoccupied with myself, my peace drains away. By moving self out of the way, I can turn the situation over to Jesus and let Him handle it.

I realize this can be a difficult and slow process. The time it takes to get rid of self depends upon your degree of hurt. It may help to remember that by giving up self you are in no way justifying the other person's behavior. You are simply following the commands of Scripture to "Bless those who persecute you; bless and do not curse … do not repay anyone evil for evil … do not avenge yourselves" (Rom. 12:14,17,19).

Think about the three people you listed on page 59. Write their initials in the following blanks.

As far as it depends on me, I will live at peace with _____.

As far as it depends on me, I will live at peace with _____.

As far as it depends on me, I will live at peace with _____.

TRY THIS TODAY

When you encounter someone who frustrates you, make a point to be especially kind to that person. Perhaps that individual really needs to be shown kindness. Consider such an opportunity a gift from the Father: a chance to put self aside, practice His love, and experience His peace.

What is God revealing to you in today's study?

_____

_____

As you close today's study, start your prayer time with this prayer:

Dear Father, Thank You for creating us. I'm giving You my people problems. Please help me see people through Your eyes and with Your love. You are the peace in all of my relationships. I love You.

Day ❸ Compassionate Living

> 📷 **Focus**: Experiencing God's peace in relationships as we learn to feel and show compassion
>
> ◣ **Scripture**: Spend a few moments with the Father as you prayerfully review Romans 12:9-21.

This week we've discussed getting self out of the way in order to experience God's peace in our relationships. One of the ways we can do this is to consider the needs of the other person.

When I taught school I realized that kids misbehaved for a reason. Maybe things were horrible at home or maybe their best friend had just lied to them or maybe they were upset about being falsely accused. Whatever the problem, I had to look deeper than their misbehavior in order to help them. I had to understand why they were behaving the way they were.

Focus on someone you know who is "misbehaving." List some things that person is doing that bother you. Be specific.

_____

You have no idea what others are going through. Each person you meet may carry a heavy burden.

Pause now in prayer. Think of a person who normally bothers you, and lift this person to the Father. Ask Him to show you how to put your feelings aside and be an encouragement to this person.

Check the examples that show what it means to bless.

○ Jess arrived at work early to get some things done before her fourth grade class came wandering in. When she got to her classroom, the cleaning staff was just beginning to clean her room. She stormed in and said, "Couldn't you guys have done this yesterday after school?"

○ It was mid-morning on the last day for the month's bills to be paid at City Hall. Janie was primed for the stampede of complaining customers who always seemed to show up at her window. Today was no different. She greeted each person warmly. If they smiled, she smiled. If they frowned, she still smiled.

○ Wanda was preparing supper after an exhausting day when the phone rang. She always answered the phone if her children were away from home, in case they needed her. Picking up the phone, she was greeted by the voice of a telemarketer. Wanda shouted into the receiver, "I wish you people would stop calling here!"

> "Bless those who persecute you; bless and do not curse."
> **Romans 12:14**

○ Doris couldn't wait for her son to get home from school. She had some exciting news to tell him about a family trip they were planning. As Jason opened the door, she blurted, "Hey, Honey! I'm so glad you're here!" Jason immediately retorted, "Mom, it's so annoying when you jump on me as soon as I walk in the door!" Doris smiled, patted his arm, and walked into the other room deciding to talk about it later.

Isn't it easy to bless those who are kind to you and pleasant to be around? On the other hand, if someone is persecuting you, you are likely experiencing pain, suffering, and great distress. These feelings may affect your physical, emotional, mental, and spiritual well-being. It takes supernatural power to bless those who are inflicting pain!

How often do you bless those who persecute you? Circle the number.

1	2	3	4	5
not at all				all the time

LEARNING HOW TO BLESS

Perhaps the Holy Spirit is creating a desire within you to bless others—
even those who are hurting you.

**Romans 12:16-21 offers excellent teaching about blessing others. Choose five
of these directives and make your own checklist. You may want to write them
on a card for quick reference throughout the day.**

1. _____

2. _____

3. _____

4. _____

5. _____

Before you can confidently "build others up," you must have the desire to
get self out of the way and love with the love of Jesus. If blessing others
becomes your goal, it becomes your ministry. Take the initiative to bless,
not to curse. You will gradually move from "It's all about me" to "It's all
about Jesus." Building others up with blessings is more than being toler-
ant of others; it's loving the way Jesus loved!

**What have you learned this week that will help you deal with stressful
relationships?**

_____

_____

As you close today's study, start your prayer time with this prayer:

*Dear Father, Please show me how to love as You love. As I grow in
the process of getting self out of the way, teach me to look for ways
to encourage others and help them discover Your love. I love You.*

Day 4 This Is My Part

> **Focus**: Focusing on Christ and heavenly things will help me love others the way Christ intends for me to love.
>
> **Scripture**: Spend a few quiet moments with the Father, asking Him to speak to you as you read Colossians 3:1-17.

Several weeks ago I was eating lunch with a friend. When the server brought a basket with three rolls in it, my friend remarked, "Why would she bring three rolls for two people? Does she want us to have it out over the third one?"

The world would tell you to stand up for yourself and take care of number one! But according to Colossians 3, that's not God's way.

GUIDELINES FOR HOLY LIVING

Paul is a great letter writer. He gives encouragement and something for the reader to hang on to. Then he fills his letters with practical applications of how we should live. Let's explore some of these standards.

1. *"Set your minds on what is above, not on what is on the earth"* (Colossians 3:2).

A distinct connection exists between getting along with others and focusing on heaven. It's difficult to focus on things above when you are being mistreated on earth! When human emotions are aroused, it takes self-restraint to focus on heaven and behave with a heavenly mindset.

Describe a time when you were mistreated and wanted to react in kind. How did you handle your emotions?

_____

_____

2. *"Put on heartfelt compassion, kindness, humility, gentleness, and patience"* (Colossians 3:12).

Is there a situation in your life right now where you can practice these things?
○ yes ○ no **Explain.**

_____

_____

Are you willing to try? ○ yes ○ no ○ not now **Why?**

_____

_____

3. *"Just as the Lord had forgiven you, so also you must forgive"*
(Colossians 3:13).

If you've been deeply wounded physically or emotionally, it is difficult to forgive—particularly if the person who hurt you has not accepted responsibility for his or her behavior. The Father knows and understands your hurt and disappointment. However, He still asks you to forgive. He wants you to forgive because it is good for you. You are in no way justifying the other person's behavior when you forgive. By letting go of your hurts, you are cleansing your heart and freeing your soul of the torment unforgiveness breeds.

God is the Righteous Judge. All people report to Him—not to you. He can create a forgiving spirit within you. Ask Him. He will bless you for your obedience.

4. *"Let the peace of the Messiah ... control your hearts"* (Colossians 3:15).

Don't you long for the peace of Jesus? As you become more intimate with the Savior, you will begin to experience His peace in indescribable ways. As you set aside a time each day to worship Him, to thank Him, to recognize Him as the Lord of your thoughts, emotions, behavior—your life—you will gradually move into a peaceful state of living. You'll find that as stressors hit, your reaction will be softened and seasoned with God's grace. It's the gift of being in His presence. It's the gentleness of Jesus. We "are being transformed into his likeness with ever-increasing glory, which comes from the Lord" (2 Corinthians 3:18, NIV).

Think of an area in your life where you are at your wit's end. The stress affects your relationships. Imagine yourself transformed into God's likeness with "ever-increasing glory." How is your situation different? Are you different? Explain.

_____

_____

5. *"Do everything in the name of the Lord Jesus"* (Colossians 3:17).

This verse has many practical applications. Right now, simply consider your relationships.

Consider your role in the relationships listed below. Write the number which best describes how frequently you "behave in the name of Jesus" in those relationships. 1 - always, 2 - usually, 3 - sometimes, 4 - rarely, 5 - never

____ husband	____ friends	____ children
____ parents	____ siblings	____ neighbors
____ acquaintances	____ coworkers	____ strangers

Did you find room for improvement? What is God revealing to you today to help you deal with people stress?

_____

_____

As you close today's study, start your prayer time with this prayer:

Dear Father, I'm beginning to see others through Your eyes. Continue to show me all You want me to know about getting along with the difficult people in my life. I belong to You. So do they. Thank You for Your love.

Day 5 Loving Others

> 📷 **Focus**: Loving others will become easier and more natural as I make sitting at the feet of Jesus a priority.
>
> 📖 **Scripture**: Read John 15. Ask the Father to fill you with the knowledge of His love.

PEOPLE CAN HURT OUR FEELINGS

During a phone conversation, a friend mentioned her church has family night suppers each week. One particular evening she and her husband ate with a group that engaged in conversation with everyone at the table except them. She described how lonely and out of place she felt.

Describe a time you felt lonely when surrounded by people.

_____

_____

HE'S PREPARING A PLACE FOR YOU

As I hurt for my friend who felt alone, I remember the words of Jesus to His disciples in John 14:2: "I am going away to prepare a place for you." Those words are not just for the disciples but are for you too! He's preparing a special place just for you where there will be no loneliness, no people competing with one another, no hurt feelings—just harmony and acceptance in Jesus.

Just imagine! When you enter the marriage feast of the Lamb, as described in Revelation 19, Jesus will be there. He is saving a place just for you. I imagine there will be much laughter and music and many conversations, but the King of Kings and Lord of Lords will offer YOU a special seat, as if you were the only one there.

According to Revelation 2:17, Christ will give you a new name written on a white stone and only known to you and Him! You will never again feel left out, unwanted, or overlooked because Jesus Himself will bring you into His presence and surround you with His love.

Read Revelation 19:6-8. List feelings that come to mind as you imagine yourself dressed in the fine white linen Christ Himself has given you to wear.

_____

Focusing on this heavenly scene, knowing it will last for eternity, helps me deal with the stress I will face until then. When I look at my "people" problems in this light, I can get through the difficult times because of Christ's love and the promise of spending forever with Him.

Following are some strategies that help me. Perhaps you'll find them useful too.

MAKE IT NOT MATTER

Sometimes people do things that hurt us. When this happens to me, I pray, "Lord just make it not matter to me." I have a tendency to get my feelings hurt easily. So when I am consumed with my self pity, I pray this prayer and believe the Lord will lift the burden of self. He does!

Describe a recent situation in your life when praying this prayer would have been helpful.

_____

_____

WALK AWAY BEFORE YOU BLOW UP

If you feel your emotions soaring and your fuse lighting, remove yourself from the situation. Walking away takes determination but is well worth the effort. When you calm down you can think more clearly, and you will have time to talk to the Lord before you speak.

How often do you walk away before you blow up in the following examples? F = frequently, O = occasionally, or S = seldom.

____ with husband   ____ with children

____ at work   ____ with strangers

DEEP BREATHE

If you begin to feel uncomfortable in a situation, take several deep breaths. This will help your blood and oxygen flow more freely to your brain and will help you think more clearly. You DO want to think before you speak, right?

Practice several deep cleansing breaths right now.

DEAL WITH YOUR NEGATIVE ATTITUDE QUICKLY

Don't allow negative thinking to find a home in your heart and mind. These disruptive thoughts can cause brain-drain. Replace them with something positive like a Scripture or pleasant thought.

Are you wasting energy by harboring negative thoughts about someone? Write two ways you can "spend" your time and energy on positive thinking.

1. _____

2. _____

IF YOU ARE WRONG, ADMIT IT QUICKLY

Admitting you are wrong shows your willingness to behave in a Christlike way. You model His compassion and forgiving nature as well.

Share a situation that could have been resolved more quickly if you had admitted you were wrong.

_____

The words Jesus spoke to YOU are recorded in John 15:3: "You are already clean because of the word I have spoken to you."

What do you think this verse means in relation to "people difficulties"?

_____

When you accepted Jesus as your Lord and Savior, He cleaned you up and filled you with His righteousness. He knows your personality, and He knows the problems you experience. If you focus on Him by worshiping Him, loving Him, and seeking His guidance, He will empower you to get along with others—no matter how difficult they may be.

What is God revealing to you during today's study?

_____

_____

As you close today's study, start your prayer time with this prayer:

Dear Father, Your love is growing inside me. I'm beginning to see people through Your eyes. Thank You. Keep me steady and seeking Your wisdom as I grow in my earthly relationships. I love You.

5

I'm Frazzled!

👄 Memory Verse

"The Lord is close to the brokenhearted and saves those who are crushed in spirit" (Psalm 34:18, NIV).

☢ Defrazzler

This week you are going to do something just for you! Plan an activity early in the week, so you can look forward to it ALL week! Anticipation is part of the fun! The only goal of this activity is to have fun and enjoy yourself.

Enjoying yourself is preventive maintenance. It's taking care of yourself. It's a way of helping you become less frazzled and frenetic. It's also a wonderful gift to your family. You're nicer when you do something just for you!

Suggestions: take a relaxing bath, get a manicure, go for a leisurely walk, go to a movie with the girls, cuddle up with a good book, eat out, go shopping.

Find something you love to do but never seem to have the time for. Remember to take notes so you can share in your group session.

☂ Weekend Mini-Retreat - John 17–20

Find a time when you can relax without feeling rushed. Experience Jesus "being with you" as you read. These are very stirring chapters. Pray you will have a fresh experience as you read. Be still before the Father. Allow Him to speak to you in a new way.

Sometime during the weekend, journal about your experience.

Day 1 My House

> 📷 **Focus**: Taking care of your body honors God
>
> 🏷 **Scripture**: Prayerfully read 1 Corinthians 6:12-20. Ask the Father what you need to do to take better care of your body.

THE PHYSICAL ATTACK OF STRESS

Eight a.m. already feels like afternoon to Janet! Before leaving for work at 6:30 a.m., she washed a load of clothes and got things ready to cook dinner for her family that evening.

Now at work, the list of things she needs to accomplish seems endless. Just thinking about the day ahead makes her exhausted. She can't imagine how she will accomplish everything that needs to be done before the end of the week.

Lately Janet's been plagued by physical problems. Her exhausted body cries out through headaches, backaches, and shoulder and neck tension, not to mention sheer depletion. Her family has noticed that she's not taking care of herself and has encouraged her to get some rest and relaxation. That sounds like good advice, but Janet feels there's simply no time to take care of her physical needs in her hectic schedule.

To what degree do you identify with Janet? Mark the continuum below.

1 ————————————— 2 ————————————— 3
not at all   somewhat   right on!

Below are physical problems many women have noticed during hectic and fast-paced days. Circle the ones you've experienced.

stomach cramps	muscle twitches
headaches	blurred vision
shortness of breath	shakiness
fatigue	unexplained rash
neck pain	jaw pain
racing pulse	other _____

GOD'S TEMPLE

First Corinthians 6:19 says, "your body is a temple of the Holy Spirit" (NIV). As I grasp that reality it becomes my personal goal to take care of my body. I love God. I love His Holy Spirit. I can honor Him by taking care of "His earthly house": my body.

Can you identify with any of the following? Check all that apply.
○ not getting enough sleep   ○ eating too much
○ rarely exercising   ○ not taking time to relax
○ not eating a balanced diet

Are any of these areas contributing to your frazzledness? If so, circle them.

It was all Libby could do to keep up with the demands at work and manage her household. Because of her busy lifestyle, she viewed an exercise program as a luxury. She hardly had enough energy to fix an evening meal, let alone exercise after a hard day at work. Already she was missing sleep by staying up late to take care of things around the house.

During lunch break Libby usually grabbed fast food while she was running errands. Sometimes she stopped at these same fast-food restaurants after work to buy supper for her family. She often resented that some women seemed to have time to exercise regularly and fix nutritious meals for their families. Those women weren't as busy as she was! Libby felt that she didn't have time to eat right, exercise, and get enough rest.

Many women feel they don't have time to take care of themselves physically. When I ask, "Why don't you take care of yourself?" in my seminars, the number one response given is "I don't have enough time!"

Do you believe God wants you to take care of your body? ○ yes ○ no
○ I've never thought about it.

In which of the following areas do you need to set goals that will help you better care for yourself physically?
○ eating   ○ sleeping   ○ exercising   ○ resting

Ignoring any one of these areas can make you tense, irritable, and unable to tackle even little things. The longer these areas go unattended, the more your body, your emotions, and your mind will suffer.

Remember 1 Corinthians 6:20? "Glorify God in your body." That's not a suggestion from Him for when you have time: it's a command straight from Scripture to take care of your physical house! Women who exercise regularly, eat nutritiously, and get enough sleep are better equipped to deal with stress on a daily basis.

This week we will continue to explore the need to take care of the spiritual house. I pray that you will approach these days with a teachable spirit, asking God to show you ways you can take better care of yourself.

What is God revealing to you through today's study?

_____

_____

As you close today's study, start your prayer time with this prayer:

Dear Father, I confess that I need to take better care of Your temple, my body. Show me how to do this. There doesn't seem to be enough time for me to take care of myself in the ways we've studied today. Show me how to honor You by taking care of my body. I love You.

Day 2 Seeking God's Guidance

> 📷 **Focus**: Following God's direction by setting goals to take better care of yourself
>
> 🪧 **Scripture**: Prayerfully read and meditate on Philippians 4:4-13. Ask God to reveal to you His desire for your physical care.

NOW OR LATER

Diane is exasperated. It is early evening, and she has just gotten home from work. Much of what she wanted to accomplish during her day at the office is still undone. She is tired, and her body is beginning to ache.

Recently Diane's doctor told her that her physical discomfort and emotional depletion were direct results of stress. He encouraged her to find a hobby and get regular exercise—anything to keep her mind off work when she wasn't there. He gave her a pamphlet about the benefits of a regular exercise program and suggested she get started right away.

"It will take a commitment of time and may even interrupt your schedule, but the benefits you will experience will be well worth the inconvenience" he said. Then came the sobering words, "If you don't start taking care of yourself now, you'll pay for it later."

Have you ever had an experience similar to Diane's? If so, briefly explain.

_____

_____

STRESS MANAGEMENT IS REALLY SELF MANAGEMENT

While it is true you can often do little about your external circumstances, you are rarely powerless to do things that will help you make it through difficult times.You are responsible for taking care of yourself by exercising, eating right, and getting enough sleep.

Do you agree with this statement? ○ yes ○ no ○ undecided Explain.

_____

Let's take a look at a typical weekday, dividing morning, afternoon, and evening hours. Beside each division, list responsibilities you have during that time. Include meals, exercise, breaks, and family time.

Morning _____

_____

Afternoon _____

_____

Evening _____

_____

Looking back at your list, answer the following questions true (T) or false (F).

____ On a typical workday, I get the proper nutrients in my diet.

____ I enjoy a regular time of Scripture study and prayer.

____ I generally get enough sleep.

____ Each day there is a time that I unwind and reflect.

____ Exercise is usually a regular part of my day.

____ At the end of the day, I usually feel frustrated and depleted.

Sometimes we don't consider the amount of stress we heap on our bodies. We must understand that stress has physical consequences. For example, if I allow stress to keep me from eating right, I may run out of steam and lose concentration.

But I *do* have control over my eating patterns. Realizing that getting the proper nutrients can affect the way I feel, look, and behave should help me want to eat properly!

Yesterday I asked you to determine areas in which you need to set some goals. I hope by now you are realizing the importance of taking care of yourself physically. By honoring God in taking care of your body, you can more effectively serve Him because you feel better.

I CAN DO ALL THINGS THROUGH CHRIST

Through our relationship with Jesus we can set manageable goals and make them a priority. Through prayer and Bible study, the Holy Spirit will lead you to set the goals God designs for you. He will also help you stick to them. "I am able to do all things through Him who strengthens me" (Philippians 4:13).

Write weekly goals for each of the areas listed on the top of page 76. Keep them simple and specific. At the end of the week, evaluate your progress. You may want to make some changes for next week or continue with the same plan. The idea is to move into a lifestyle of taking care of yourself physically. (I've included examples in each area to help you get started.)

Exercise: Four days next week, I will walk briskly for 20 minutes.
Diet/nutrition: I will snack on fruit instead of candy.
Sleep/rest: I will take 10 minutes every afternoon to deep breathe and get my mind off work.

Prayerfully seek the Lord's guidance in each goal you set.

Exercise:

1. _____

2. _____

Diet/nutrition:

1. _____

2. _____

Sleep/rest:

1. _____

2. _____

What is God revealing to you during today's study?

_____

_____

As you close today's study, start your prayer time with this prayer:

Dear Father, Thank You for caring for my physical needs and for helping me make these goals priorities in my life. Give me a spirit of excitement about this part of my journey with You! I love You.

Day 3 The Stress of Sin

📷 **Focus**: Harboring unconfessed sin can cause much stress.

📖 **Scripture**: Prayerfully read Psalm 32. Thank the Father for forgiving all of your sins.

OUT OF FELLOWSHIP

Donna often recalls the unrest she experienced several years ago. She remembers the day she went to her doctor because of shortness of breath, heart palpitations, and other physical discomforts. After an examination, her doctor asked, "Are you under some kind of stress?"

Donna was suffering from the weight of unconfessed sin in her life. She didn't admit it at the time, but she now realizes that being out of harmony with God affected her emotionally, mentally, and physically. God has used this experience to allow her to help others recognize the damaging effects of unconfessed sin.

We have discussed the importance of taking care of yourself physically. Not attending to your physical needs can contribute to unwanted stress in your life. A complacent attitude toward sinful behavior can also lead to stress overload.

Consider some damaging effects of unconfessed sin. Circle those you or someone you know has experienced.

sleeplessness	lack of energy	inability to focus
loss of appetite	racing pulse	restlessness
loss of joy	physical aches	lack of interest in things
withdrawal from people	distraction	other _____

David knew the agony of unconfessed sin (see Psalm 32:3-4 in margin). Before giving his sin to God, he experienced a spiritual drought and heaviness. God does not want you to settle for anything less than a full and abundant life with Him. "I have come that they may have life and have it in abundance" (John 10:10).

When we are involved in personal sin, God will allow us to experience great physical, emotional, and mental discomfort. Discomfort is part of the refining process, drawing our wayward hearts back to Him. He is always working out His plan for our lives and is consistently leading us to the place of contentment and joy in His presence.

> "When I kept silence [before I confessed,] my bones wasted away through my groaning all the day long. For day and night Your hand [of displeasure] was heavy upon me; my moisture was turned into the drought of summer."
> **Psalm 32:3-4, AMP**

RATIONALIZING SINS

Not until Donna's doctor asked if she were under some type of stress, did Donna come to terms with a particular sin area in her life. Prior to the doctor's question, she had shrugged off her sin as no big deal.

Unconfessed sin creates a barrier between you and God. Since the fall in the Garden of Eden, sin has been a reality for all of

God's children. To rationalize sin and deny its existence in your life is to deny the truth of Scripture. "If we say 'We have no sin,' we are deceiving ourselves, and the truth is not in us" (1 John 1:8).

Therefore, we need to acknowledge the reality of sin and the need to confess. We don't have to live with the burden of unconfessed sin. God has promised to completely forgive us and restore our joy. "If we confess our sins, He is faithful and righteous to forgive us our sins and to cleanse us from all unrighteousness" (1 John 1:9).

Physical suffering is not always indicative of unconfessed sin in our lives, and many other causes lead to sickness. However, since we are focusing on things that cause us to be frazzled and stressed, we need to take a look at the unconfessed sin issue.

In Psalm 32:3-4, David described what he experienced before he acknowledged his sin. Have you experienced that kind of anguish?
○ yes ○ no **If yes, explain how this event brought you closer to God.**

_____

_____

Feelings of sadness, guilt, anger, embarrassment, shame, and despair are experienced as consequences of sin. God does not desire that you stay in a place of hurt, but He will allow you to experience these emotions to bring you to repentance. You may need to repent of an attitude or a behavior or even a lifestyle that is displeasing to Him. God will not allow you to experience His peace if you are living out of His will.

GOD'S FORGIVENESS IS COMPLETE

As I read David's words in Psalm 32:5, I can almost feel the physical breaking of chains. I sense a weight lifted and a burden dropped. David's words point to the joy we experience when we come clean before the Lord.

"Then I acknowledged my sin to You, and did not cover up my iniquity. I said, 'I will confess my transgressions to the Lord'—and You forgave the guilt of my sin" (Psalm 32:5, NIV).

Spend a few moments in prayer, asking God to reveal any area in your life that is causing a barrier between you and Him. Ask Him what you need to do. Commit to be obedient and accept His instruction. Make notes of what actions you think He's calling you to take.

What is God revealing to you today?

_____

_____

As you close today's study, start your prayer time with this prayer:

Dear Father, Thank You for loving me. Search my heart. Reveal any attitude, thought, or behavior that is not pleasing to You. Give me the desire to live in obedience to You in every way. Be my strength, Lord. I love You.

Day 4 Clean Before God

📷 **Focus**: Experiencing the joy of being forgiven

📖 **Scripture**: As you read Psalm 34, ask God to fill you with the joy of your salvation.

DIFFICULTY ACCEPTING GOD'S FORGIVENESS

Marie's childhood and teenage years were traumatic and filled with shameful memories. She blames herself for the horrible things that happened to her— though there was little, if anything, she could have done to prevent them from happening. She feels she doesn't deserve God's love and forgiveness.

Camille, on the other hand, grew up in a Christian environment and invited Jesus into her heart at an early age. She loves the Lord and has experienced many years of walking closely with Him. However, her intimacy with the Lord changed when she fell into deep sin that caused her to feel she was totally unworthy of God's love and forgiveness.

Marie and Camille are both Christians who feel unworthy of God's love.

**Have you ever felt you didn't deserve God's love ? ○ yes ○ no
If so, describe your feelings.**

_____

How do you feel about the forgiveness of your sins?

○ I believe I'm forgiven.

○ Because of things I've done I sometimes wonder if God really can forgive my sins.

○ I sometimes try to work harder at "being good" to make up for my sins.

○ There are some sins I don't think God can forgive.

○ I really do want to believe that I'm forgiven, but I'm having a hard time accepting it.

WHEN THE RIGHTEOUS CRY FOR HELP

If you are a child of God, you are righteous. You have invited Jesus into your heart and because of that, you are in right standing with God. Your position in Him has nothing to do with effort. It's all about the price Jesus paid for your sin. You are righteous not because of who you are but because of who He is!

Prayerfully meditate on Psalm 34:17. Then answer the following questions. What two things does the Lord do when the righteous cry out for help?

1. _____

2. _____

Are you righteous? (see earlier definition) ○ **yes** ○ **no**

Fill in these blanks.

I am _____ before God because of what Jesus did for me on

the cross. Therefore, when I cry out to Him, He will _____

me and deliver me from my _____.

What an incredible reality! I cry out to the Lord in my sorrow and He lovingly delivers me from all the distress I feel! According to Psalm 34:18 of The Amplified Bible, "The Lord is close to those who are of a broken heart and saves such as are crushed in spirit." The Amplified Bible defines *crushed in spirit* as, "crushed with sorrow for sin and humbly and thoroughly penitent."

You will never be worthy of God's blessings. You will never deserve the forgiveness of God. You can only humbly accept and appreciate His forgiveness and be in awe of His extravagant love for you. When you let the reality of that truth grab you, you won't be able to stop praising Him! You'll want to cry out, "Glorify the LORD with me; let us exalt his name together" (Psalm 34:3, NIV)!

Take a few moments to praise God for His extravagant love. Sing to Him with your voice or in your heart. Worship Him and thank Him. Rejoice in Him!

One way you can show your thankfulness for God's gift of grace is to develop a lifestyle of continual praise and gratitude. "I will bless the Lord at all times; His praise shall continually be in my mouth" (Psalm 34:1, AMP).

Schedule two opportunities to praise God today in ways or at times you don't usually praise Him. Write them below.

1. _____

2. _____

What is God revealing to you today?

_____

_____

As you close today's study, start your prayer time with this prayer:

Dear Father, I can't thank You enough for Your love for me. I offer You the praise of my mouth today. Your mercy and lovingkindness are more than I can imagine and more than I deserve. Thank You. I love You so much!

Day 5 My Identity

> 📷 **Focus**: Defining your self worth through your relationship with Jesus Christ, even when life is stressful
>
> 📖 **Scripture**: As you read Isaiah 61:10-11, spend a few moments thinking about your righteousness in Jesus Christ.

WHO AM I?

Bonnie was in the middle of the wellness seminar her supervisor had asked her to attend. She had looked forward to taking a break from phones, computers, and clients, and she enjoyed learning how to deal with stress and begin an exercise program. But the instructor had asked the participants to do something that was a little more difficult for Bonnie. "Write a brief paragraph describing who you are."

The more Bonnie considered the question, the more confused she became. She could describe what she looked like. She could tell "who" she was at work. She could describe her roles of wife and mother, but none of those descriptions explained who she was.

Perplexed and a bit disturbed, Bonnie began to ponder more deeply the question, "Who am I?"

If you identify with Bonnie's confusion in trying to answer "Who am I?" the following statements may help you take a closer look at how you view yourself. Answer true (T) or false (F) according to what's for you!

_____ People usually recognize me as my children's mother.

_____ My self worth is often based on my performance at work.

_____ When I "look good," I feel better about myself.

_____ If my house were clean and organized, I would feel better about myself.

_____ People know me by what I do.

_____ I'm usually known as my husband's wife.

_____ I often compare myself with women who are successful in business.

_____ When someone wants to know about me, I usually respond by telling them what I do, where I go to church, where I live, and how many children I have.

_____ I regularly think of myself as being a child of God.

HOW GOD VIEWS YOU

Read what Isaiah 61:10 (NIV) says God has done for you. Then fill in the blanks.

He has clothed you with garments of _____ and arrayed you

with the robe of _____!

Colossians 3:3 says. "your [new, real] life is hidden with Christ in God" (AMP). That new life has nothing to do with what we do or who we are, but with our position in Christ. Women who are going through particularly stressful times often lose sight of their identity. Notice that I did not say they lose their identity, but they lose sight of it! When you experience failure or inadequacy in a particular area of life, it's easy to define your self-worth or self-esteem within the context of that area.

In which of the following areas do you often base your identity and determine your self-worth? Check all that apply.

○ my job performance   ○ being a mother
○ my work in the church   ○ being a wife
○ how well I keep house   ○ how I look
○ my intelligence   ○ the approval of others
○ other _____

To what degree do you define your self-esteem based on your "performance" in any of these areas? Circle one.

rarely   pretty often   most of the time

THE DAUGHTER OF THE KING

God has clothed you in royal attire! Paul says in 2 Corinthians 5:20 that we are Christ's ambassadors. The spiritual world sees you wearing your royal garments. Your identity is in Christ, not in what you do or who you are.

When you see yourself this way, you will shout with the prophet Isaiah, "I delight greatly in the LORD; my soul rejoices in my God. For he has clothed me with garments of salvation and arrayed me in a robe of righteousness" (Isaiah 61:10, NIV).

Do you walk, talk, and behave as if you are dressed in royal garments?

○ absolutely   ○ every now and then   ○ are you kidding?

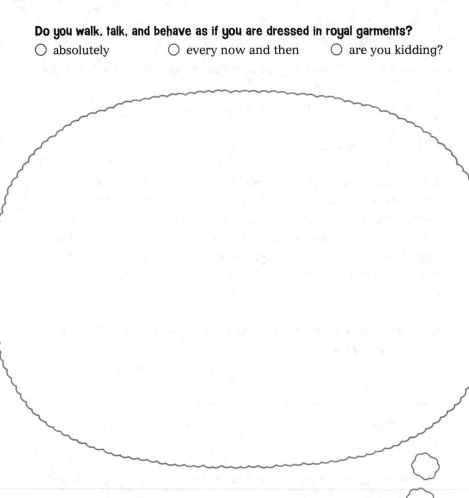

In the thougt balloon above, draw yourself dressed in your royal attire. Try to think of other symbols of royalty besides the ones we've mentioned.

After you've finished your drawing answer the following questions.

If you were to think of yourself as clothed in royal attire, would you carry yourself differently in the grocery store, at the bank, in your neighborhood? ○ yes ○ no ○ I'd be the same.

How might viewing yourself as "royalty" affect the way you interact with others?

_____

_____

As you focus on wearing your royal robes, consider the following physical tips that will help you express the reality of your spiritual nature.

- Smile. This helps others feel comfortable and often opens the door for you to share Jesus.
- Stand tall. Look confident. Christ died for YOU. Present an image that shows you are thankful for His sacrifice.
- Look people in the eye. This shows genuine interest and sensitivity.
- Groom yourself well. Pay attention to details like your fingernails, hair, cleanliness of clothes.
- Take deep breathing breaks. This will help you remain calm when stressors hit.
- Think of others first. Show you are interested by listening intently and asking questions. Put the other person's needs before your own.
- Remain positive. Remember you have a positive God!

What is God revealing to you today?

_____

_____

As you close today's study, start your prayer time with this prayer:

Dear Father, Help me see myself today as You see me. I love You.

6

Near to the Heart of God

👄 Memory Verse

"You have revealed the paths of life to me; You will fill me with gladness in Your presence" (Acts 2:28).

☢ Defrazzler

Plan a time this week to take a leisurely, relaxing walk with God. Let this be a time you look forward to and talk to Him about. Ask God to bless the time you set aside to take a walk with Him. Ask Him to prepare your heart to experience His love in an extravagant way.

Carry a Scripture card of Acts 2:28 on your walk. Ask God to fill you with His joy and presence as you turn your heart to Him. Get excited about what He is doing in your life. Praise Him. Sing to Him. Love Him.

Be ready to share about your experience with your small group.

☂ Weekend Mini-Retreat - John 21

Relax and enjoy this last chapter of John. Notice how Jesus continues to reveal Himself to His disciples, talking with them and meeting their physical and spiritual needs.

Ask Him to meet your needs in a deeply personal way. Just as Jesus did long ago to His early disciples, He longs to reveal Himself to you. His longing to give far surpasses your ability to receive. Open your heart to Him and allow Him to bless you.

Take some time during the weekend to record your reflections.

Day ✿ The Faith Test

> 📷 **Focus**: Basing my faith on my position in Jesus Christ, not on the way I feel
>
> 🕮 **Scripture**: As you read Matthew 14:22-33, consider God's gift of faith to you. Ask Him to strengthen your faith in Him.

Have you ever felt you couldn't pass the faith test? You've prayed, read your Bible, and fasted, yet you still lack faith. What you're experiencing may have nothing to do with faith and everything to do with feelings.

Today we will take a look at the reality of faith and how our feelings can divert our attention from Jesus.

CONFUSION DURING THE STORM

Peter had walked with Jesus long enough to experience His love, tenderness, and mighty power. He had listened intently to the parables about the farmer sowing his seeds, the mustard seed, and the net full of fish. He had seen Jesus miraculously feeding the 5,000 people who had followed Him. Peter experienced many miracles in the presence of Jesus, and the Master gave him authority to drive out evil spirits and heal diseases. How then, after walking on the water in those first few steps of faith, did Peter lose sight of Jesus and begin to sink?

What are some great events you have experienced during your walk with the Lord? Circle all that apply. Add others you think of that aren't listed.

the birth of a baby	a loved one saved	a sunrise
unexplainable peace	answered prayers	joy in the midst of trials
deliverance from sin	divine guidance	other _____

Can you, like Peter, testify to God's goodness in your life? ○ yes ○ no
Can you also identify with Peter's experience of focusing on the storm around him, instead of keeping his focus on Jesus? ○ yes ○ no

Notice I said, "Peter's experience of focusing on the storm" and not, "Peter's loss of faith." Faith is a product of the spirit. Romans 12:3 says

God has apportioned faith to each of us. If you are a child of God, it is in your spiritual nature to have faith.

At times, however, you might confuse your feelings with your faith. Satan uses doubt and unbelief to make you think you have to work hard to have faith. And when you just can't seem to work hard enough, he tells you your faith is lacking. The problem is not your lack of faith, it's Satan seeking to destroy your faith with lies.

BASING FAITH ON GOD'S WORD, NOT ON FEELINGS

God provided Amy with a new job. He gave her the desire, the faith, and the ability to do her work well. She knew when she accepted the job that it was a gift from God.

Now things are happening that make it difficult for her to enjoy her work as she once did. She is beginning to doubt and question herself, wondering if she really heard from God in the first place. Is this really the job He has for her?

Describe an experience when you knew God was speaking to you.

_____

Did you later wonder if you really DID hear Him? If so, describe how you felt.

_____

"For I know the plans I have for you," declares the LORD, "plans to prosper you and not to harm you, plans to give you hope and a future." Jeremiah 29:11, NIV

God places dreams and visions within your heart. When He gives you a particular calling, He will also give you the desire, faith, and ability to carry through. He may call you to start a new job, teach a Bible study, or begin a family.

Whatever God has called you to do in faith, whether it's trusting Him with the life of your child or trusting Him with your finances, He wants you to know that He has your best interest at heart. He provides for your every need.

Place a check beside the statements you believe.
- ⭘ God loves me.
- ⭘ God will never leave me.
- ⭘ God wants the best for me.
- ⭘ God's will for my life is best.

Remember our study of Abraham in week 1? God made him a promise and many years later he had not seen the results. However, Abraham stood in faith. He must have been attacked by doubts and unbelief, but according to Scripture he stood steadfast and unmovable. "No unbelief *or* distrust made him waver (doubtingly question) concerning the promise of God, but he grew strong *and* was empowered by faith as he gave praise *and* glory to God" (Romans 4:20, AMP).

During his time of waiting and watching and hoping that God's promise would come to pass, Abraham kept praising and giving glory to God! As he did he grew stronger and became empowered. Perhaps, unlike Peter, who placed his mind on the storm at hand instead of focusing on the Master, Abraham just praised God and gave God glory for who He was!

Place an X on the line indicating to what degree you are like Peter or Abraham.

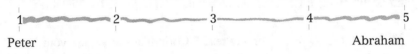

1   2   3   4   5

Peter   Abraham

DON'T BE THROWN OFF COURSE

Storms, doubts, and confusion can intimidate you. In times of trial, feelings are unpredictable and unreliable. But choosing to have faith in God has little to do with how you feel! Don't allow feelings of worry, doubt, and confusion to keep you from experiencing the peace God wants you to enjoy as you rest in His presence.

Let's look once more at what Abraham did when the wait got long. "No unbelief *or* distrust made him waver (doubtingly question) concerning the promise of God, but he grew strong *and* was empowered by faith as he gave praise *and* glory to God" (Romans 4:20, AMP).

"Come to Me, all you who labor and are heavy-laden and overburdened, and I will cause you to rest. [I will ease and relieve and refresh your souls]." **Matthew 11:28, AMP**

List two circumstances you've prayed about and given to the Lord many times but still haven't received an answer for.

1. _____

2. _____

Are you willing to keep praising God, giving Him glory as you wait it out?
○ yes ○ no

As you close today's study, start your prayer time with this prayer:

Dear Father, My heart's desire is to trust You. I'm determining to praise
You as I wait for You to show me how You are working in this situation.
Help me keep my eyes focused on You—not on my doubts and confusions.
May I bring glory to You as I wait before You. I love You.

Day 2 More Than a Case of the Blues *(Part One)*

> 📷 **Focus**: Being a Christian doesn't make you immune to difficulties.
>
> 📖 **Scripture**: As you prayerfully read 2 Corinthians 5:1-8, ask your
> Father to help you remember that your body may be fragile, but
> His Spirit living within you is not!

Have you ever been unable to shake the blues? You keep trying and trying
but you can't quite seem to feel better?

I have such a heart for this topic. Before experiencing depression
myself, I had no understanding of the debilitating effects of the illness.
Being a committed Christian with a close relationship with the Lord, I felt
I could pray my way out of anything. As pressures stacked up in my life,
I disciplined myself to increase my prayer time.

But as weeks turned into months, my physical, emotional, and mental
condition spiraled downward. I felt guilty and helpless as I desperately
tried to get a grip on my life. It never occurred to me that I was getting
first-hand experience on how to deal with and later teach about clinical
depression.

Can you recall a time when you had the "blues" that wouldn't let go? ○ **yes**
○ **no If so, describe your experience.**

_____

_____

Did you try to do something to make the blues go away? ○ yes ○ no
If so, describe your effort.

_____

Were you successful? ○ yes ○ no Explain.

_____

MEANWHILE WE GROAN

In 2 Corinthians Paul often refers to his frail and abused body. In today's passage, he speaks of the burden he carries within his body and how he longs to be in his permanent dwelling place. Have you ever felt the "burden" of your body, mind, and emotions? Have you longed for your permanent place in heaven where the demands of life will be gone?

"What is mortal may be swallowed up" (2 Corinthians 5:4, NIV). His Spirit serves as a "deposit, guaranteeing what is to come" (2 Corinthians 5:5, NIV). One day you will be far removed from the pressures of life.

Until then, you live in a physical body that is designed for life on earth. Your body contains blood vessels, muscles, tissues, organs, ligaments, and various operating systems. Intricately and delicately designed, your body is your earthly tent and is susceptible to earthly wear and tear.

The body doesn't work one way for Christians and another way for non-Christians. Loving the Lord does not mean you will be immune to the attack of stressors on your body, mind, and emotions.

Describe a circumstance in your life that you expected to be stress-free because of your relationship with the Lord.

_____

GUILT FEELINGS

When I finally broke down (literally) and went to my doctor for help, he asked me about stress issues in my life. He wanted to know what kind of pressures I was under, and how long I had been experiencing them.

As I described the nature of my stress and the symptoms I was experiencing, I realized I was pretty bad off. I had never admitted the severity of my problem and certainly had never shared it with anyone else. (We will discuss symptoms of depression later in our study.)

I will always be grateful for my doctor's words: "First of all, don't feel guilty." Hearing that statement helped me release the feelings of guilt I had been experiencing and begin my healing process. I later learned many Christians who suffer from clinical depression experience this kind of guilt.

Why do you think many Christians feel guilty about feeling depressed?

I feel the need to go slowly and prayerfully as we explore this sensitive area. If you have not experienced a time of depression in your life, chances are you will. If not, then perhaps someone close to you will. Developing a spiritual viewpoint on this sickness will help you to respond in a biblical way.

GOD IS CLOSE TO YOU

Psalm 34:18 offered much hope and strength to me during my dark days. "The LORD is near the brokenhearted; He saves those crushed in spirit." When I stopped trying to work my way out, I began to rest in the reality of His closeness. I began to yearn for and crave His presence in my brokenness. What a comfort He was to me!

Thank your Father now for being close to you when you are brokenhearted.

We will continue to explore the subject of depression this week. Ask the Father to give you sensitivity for those going through a difficult time.

If *you* are experiencing the blues that won't go away, be assured that Jesus loves you, and you are never out of His loving gaze. Be "full of good and hopeful and confident courage" (2 Corinthians 5:6, AMP). He will save your crushed spirit!

As you close today's study, start your prayer time with this prayer:

Dear Father, Thank You for never leaving me and for being close to me when I am brokenhearted. Thank You for the assurance that though my body is weak, my spirit is strong. For You reside in my spirit. You are my joy and my strength. I love You.

Day ❸ More Than a Case of the Blues *(Part Two)*

> 📷 **Focus**: Gaining a better understanding of depression
>
> 🔖 **Scripture**: As you read Isaiah 40:28-31, thank God for His unfailing love and for His desire to renew your strength.

Diana was trying to believe what she was reading in her morning devotional. The phrases from Isaiah kept staring back at her from her Bible: *soar on wings like eagles, run and not grow weary, walk and not be faint.* It had been some time since she had gotten excited about the promises of Scripture. In fact, she seemed to never have any excitement or joy about anything these days. Things that used to bring her happiness and fulfillment, like going places with her family, now only made her feel tired and bogged down. Everything was an effort and nothing seemed to bring her pleasure the way it used to. As Diana read Isaiah's verses again, she couldn't help wondering, *If God gives strength to the weary, why do I feel so tired and so rotten about life?*

Does anything in Diana's story ring a bell with you? ○ yes ○ no
If yes, explain.

_____

_____

GOD KNOWS AND WILL GIVE UNDERSTANDING

Not understanding what's happening with your body, your mind, or your emotions can be exasperating and unsettling. God knows and cares about your frustration! "The LORD is the everlasting God, the Creator of the ends of the earth. He will not grow tired or weary, and his understanding no one can fathom. He gives strength to the weary and increases the power of the weak" (Isaiah 40:28-29, NIV).

One way He increases the power of the weak is by increasing their understanding. If I understand more about how my body functions, perhaps I can more readily believe that the God who controls all the parts of my body is also in control of every frustration I have concerning my body.

Is there an area in your life where you need God to give you understanding?
○ yes ○ no If so, what is it?

_____

Pause and pray to your Father about the understanding you seek. Thank Him for the truth recorded in Isaiah 41:10.

CHEMICALS AND THE BRAIN

The brain is housed in one of the most intricate systems in the body: the central nervous system. Just as the parts of a machine are subject to wear and tear, so too are the parts of our body systems prone to breakdown. In my depression, my brain became the faulty part.

My doctor explained it this way: "When you go through a stressful situation for a long period of time, the chemicals in your brain may begin to alter. When that happens, the chemicals that were once balanced become unbalanced and you could enter into a period of depression." I later learned that depression can also be caused by medication, or other medical illnesses, certain personalities, or family history.

I found it tremendously helpful to know there was a "medical" reason for what I was experiencing. The Lord used that doctor's visit to provide understanding, so I could begin the recovery process.

LOOKING AT THE SYMPTOMS OF DEPRESSION

Today's study is not intended to give you medical advice. I am not equipped to offer treatment plans or to tell you what should be done if you or a loved one is experiencing depression. But I can offer you insight into this sickness by looking at its common symptoms and encouraging you to seek medical attention if the symptoms are persistent.

If you are daily experiencing five or more of the following symptoms for more than a two-week period, it's likely you're struggling with depression.

"So do not fear, for I am with you; do not be dismayed, for I am your God. I will strengthen you and help you; I will uphold you with my righteous right hand."
Isaiah 41:10, NIV

- extreme feelings of sadness and a depressed mood
- loss of interest and pleasure in spending time with family and friends
- significant changes in appetite
- sleeping too much or too little
- feelings of guilt, hopelessness, or worthlessness
- inability to make decisions, focus, and remember
- constant fatigue and lack of energy
- restlessness, decreased activity
- thoughts of suicide or death

If you suspect depression, make an appointment with your doctor. If you or someone you know is having thoughts of suicide, seek professional help immediately.

SO WHAT NOW?

If you are experiencing depression, you must take care of yourself before healing can begin. Prayerfully consider these suggestions.

- Slow down. Don't try to do as much as you are accustomed to doing.
- Don't take on new activities.
- Delegate some of your responsibilities.
- Be kind to yourself when you can't accomplish what you normally accomplish.
- Plan additional time to relax during each day.
- Don't load your weekend with housework or other "catch up" activities.
- Eat a well-balanced diet.
- Get enough sleep.
- Cut out some night activities.
- Refrain from making major decisions.
- Seek comfort from family and friends who love you.
- Spend quiet time with the Lord, resting in His presence, thinking about how much He loves you, being confident He will renew your strength.

Prayerfully seek the Father's direction, asking Him if you need to commit to any area(s) on this list. Place a check by each area of commitment. Trust Him. He will reveal what you need to do and He'll give you the strength to do it.

Has the Father brought anyone to mind who may need help dealing with depression? If so, write that person's name (or initials) here. _____

If you wrote your name, will you be open to the Father's direction and make an appointment with your doctor if that's His desire? ○ yes ○ no

If you wrote the name of a friend in the blank will you commit to pray for that friend and offer comfort, encouragement, and information from this study as the Father leads? ○ yes ○ no

As you close today's study, start your prayer time with this prayer:

Dear Lord, Thank You so much for the strength of Your presence. Thank You for making my body in such an intricate and wonderful way. I praise You for Your mighty works. I want to soar on wings like eagles and run and not grow weary. I put my hope in You. I love You.

Day 4 The Faith Test

> ◉ **Focus**: Understanding God does not condemn you when you become weary and worn out. He rushes to meet your needs.
>
> 🔖 **Scripture**: Prayerfully read 1 Kings 18–19. Don't rush. Allow the Father to speak to you as you learn about a great man of God who experienced deep discouragement and depression.

The Father has used the portrait of Elijah in 1 Kings time and again to encourage and assure me of His presence in my circumstances. Elijah's life is the picture of one who gave his all in service to the Lord. Then, depleted and worn, he tired and begged God to let him die.

After God showed His glory and power in a contest with the prophets of Baal, Elijah expected a quick destruction of evil. However, the evil system of Jezebel and her followers did not immediately crumble. Instead of pardoning Elijah or begging for mercy, she threatened to hunt him down and kill him by the next day. This news shattered the prophet's confidence. He fled the region, plunging deeply into the desert where he collapsed under a juniper tree.

When Elijah thought he had no reason to live and nothing else to give, the Lord came to him and ministered to his weary soul. He sent Elijah back out with the promise to protect him and all those who had not bowed to Baal.

ELIJAH WAS AFRAID AND RAN FOR HIS LIFE

Being instrumental in revealing God's glory at the showdown between the "one true God" and Baal had to be the spiritual high of Elijah's life!

Describe a mountaintop experience when you were an instrument God used to reveal His glory. (His glory may have been revealed to one or many.)

_____

Could the Elijah in 1 Kings 19:3 be the same Elijah who called down fire from the Lord in 1 Kings 18? Elijah was not a coward, but he was weary and ran away from the intensity of life. He was at a spiritual low point, just after experiencing a spiritual high point! This servant felt like running, and he did! When Queen Jezebel threatened to take his life, he fled the scene.

At times we all feel like fleeing. We deal with stressors fairly well until one sends us over the edge. It may be our inability to handle these stressors has more to do with the accumulation of stressors than the stressor itself.

What events have made you flee the scene physically, mentally, or emotionally in your past? Check all that apply.
- ○ problems with teenagers
- ○ financial worries
- ○ responsibilities with parents
- ○ loss of a loved one
- ○ marital problems
- ○ a new job
- ○ physical pain
- ○ other _____

What did you want God to do in your circumstance?

_____

ELIJAH LOST SIGHT OF GOD

Elijah's words reveal how he viewed himself, others, and God at this time in his life. "I have been very zealous for the LORD God Almighty. The Israelites have rejected your covenant, broken down your altars, and put your prophets to death with the sword. I am the only one left, and now they are trying to kill me too" (1 Kings 19:10, NIV).

Elijah saw himself as the only one still faithful to the Lord. He had become self-centered and self-pitying. He was comparing his works to the works of others. And although he doesn't specifically admit it, his words imply he no longer trusted God to take care of his safety.

Describe a time you felt you were the only one being faithful to God.

_____

WE WANT GOD TO FIX OTHER PEOPLE AND CIRCUMSTANCES

Based on his feelings of discouragement, Elijah assumed his fruitfulness for God and his ministry were over. He wanted a quick fix from God. After all, wasn't this the same God who revealed His awesomeness in a blast of glory? So why wouldn't He destroy Jezebel and her wicked kingdom?

**Have you ever asked God, "Why don't you go ahead and ...? ○ yes ○ no
If so, did you get the answer you wanted? ○ yes ○ no Explain.**

_____

GOD SPOKE IN THE SILENCE

Review 1 Kings 19:11-14. This passage speaks directly to my heart's need to hear from God. Many times when I pour out my longings to God, He gives me His presence instead of my desire of the moment.

That's what happened with Elijah. After the wind, earthquake, and fire, there came a gentle whisper. And through that whisper, God spoke!

God did reveal himself in wind (Job 38:1, AMP), earthquakes (Exodus 19:18, NIV), and fire (1 Kings 18:38, NIV) at other points in Scripture, but it is significant that at this moment, God spoke through a whisper.

God was teaching the discouraged prophet a bold and powerful truth. I imagine He was saying, "When things don't go the way you want or the way you expect, continue to trust Me. Let Me be God. Let Me do things My way. I know what I'm doing. I will take care of you."

Is there a circumstance in your life in which you are longing for God to intervene with His power and might? Are you tired and weary in life's struggles? Will you "fall under the juniper tree" and allow God to minister to you, soothe you, and speak to you in His still, small voice?

What is God revealing to you during today's study?

_____

_____

As you close today's study, start your prayer time with this prayer:

Dear Father, Sometimes I'm restless and long to hear Your gentle voice. I've had wonderful mountaintop experiences with You, and I thank You so much for allowing Your presence to fill my life. I also thank You for the times when life seems difficult, and I'm not sure of Your plans for me. It is during these times You reveal Your presence to me in unspeakable ways. Thank You for being with me during the spiritual highs and lows. Continue to fill me with Your presence. I love You.

Day 5 Jesus Is Praying for You

> **Focus**: Grasping the awesome reality that Jesus, your Savior, talks to the Father about YOU
>
> **Scripture**: Read John 17:1-26. Ask the Father to open your eyes to the truth of His Word as you position yourself to receive the wonder of His love.

It's hard to believe we are at the end of our study! The Father has blessed me immeasurably during this time of research, study, prayer, and seeking His guidance. What a challenging journey it has been. Many times during these months, He called me to my knees to pray for you. And what a privilege it has been!

My desire as I write this material is to grow in my intimacy with Jesus, so I can bring glory to Him in every thought, attitude, and emotion. My passion, my prayer, my goal is to help you grow in your intimacy with the Father. I long for you to want to know Him more than anything in life.

With "1" being your level of intimacy when you began this study and "5" being significant growth, how would you measure this study's impact on your spiritual growth?

1━━━━━━2━━━━━━3━━━━━━4━━━━━━5

Check the statements on page 100 that describe your thoughts as we come to the end of our study.

○ Studying the Scriptures and spending time with Jesus have increased my love for Him and my desire to know more about Him.
○ I look forward to spending time with Him each day.
○ The more I learn about Him, the more I want to learn about Him.
○ Building my relationship with Jesus Christ is helping me better deal with the stresses of life.
○ I believe Jesus wants "being with Him" to be my number one priority.
○ My heart is filled with worship and praise as I think about God's love for me.
○ I crave His presence throughout the day.

As you grow in your love for the Lord, you can experience His joy each step of the way. It's gradual work. The Scripture says joy comes "from one degree of glory to another" (2 Cor. 3:18, AMP). Each day can bring a new degree of glory as you choose to grow in your walk with Him.

As you grow, it's important for you to realize Jesus is praying for you! Let the reality of that statement get a hold on you! The King of Kings and Lord of Lords is lifting YOU to His Father in prayer!

Today you read John 17, the prayer Jesus prayed shortly before He died on the cross. A theme runs through this chapter about a gift given to Jesus.

Review John 17:1-26. What does the prayer of Jesus have to do with a gift? (verses 6,9,24 will give you specific clues)

_____

Who gave the gift? _____

Who received the gift? _____

Who IS the gift? _____

I love John 17:24 of The Amplified Bible: "Father, I desire that they also whom You have entrusted to Me [as Your gift to Me] may be with Me."

Have you ever considered that you are a love-gift to Jesus from the Father?
○ yes ○ never

Think of the most wonderful gift you've ever received and remember the joy and gratefulness you felt upon receiving it. Multiply that feeling infinitely and you will catch a glimpse of how Jesus feels about you: God's love-gift.

Does viewing yourself as a gift from the Father cause you to feel differently about your relationship with Jesus? ○ yes ○ no **Explain.**

_____

Personalize the prayer of Jesus so you can grasp the reality of His great love for you as He prays for you. Write your name in each blank. Enjoy this activity. Go slowly and let the reality sink in that Jesus, the Savior, talks to God, the Father, about you!

"I pray for _____. I am not praying for the world, but for _____ you have given me, for _____ [is] yours. All I have is yours, and all you have is mine. And glory has come to me through _____. I am coming to you now, but I say these things while I am still in the world, so that _____ may have the full measure of my joy within [her]. My prayer is not that you take _____ out of the world but that you protect [her] from the evil one. _____ [is] not of the world, even as I am not of it. Sanctify _____ by the truth; your word is truth. As you sent me into the world, ⊠I have sent _____ into the world. For _____, I sanctify myself, that _____ too may be truly sanctified. Righteous Father, though the world does not know you, I know you, and _____ know[s] that you have sent me. I have made you known to _____, and will continue to make you known in order that the love you have for me may be in _____ and that I myself may be in _____" (John 17:9-10,13,15-19,25-26, NIV).

INTIMACY AND JESUS

We began this study talking about how Martha stayed busy when Jesus came to visit, but Mary dropped everything and sat with Him. We're closing it with the realization that Jesus is praying for us to grow in our relationship with Him. I pray that as you continue to grow in your love for the Lord, you will keep yearning to explore the benefits of "coming out of the kitchen and sitting at the feet of Jesus."

As you close today's study, start your prayer time with this prayer:

Dear Father, Thank You for being intent on becoming intimate with me. I continue to be overwhelmed by Your love for me and with the reality that You pray for me. Thank You for being my personal Lord and Savior and the absolute Lord of my life. I truly do love You.

❀ HOW TO BECOME A CHRISTIAN ❀

God wants us to love Him above anyone or anything else because loving Him puts everything else in life in perspective. In God we find the hope, peace, and joy that are possible only through a personal relationship with Him. Through His presence in our lives, we can truly love others, because God is love.

John 3:16 says, " 'God loved the world in this way: He gave His One and Only Son, so that everyone who believes in Him will not perish but have eternal life.' " In order to live our earthly lives "to the full" (John 10:10, NIV), we must accept God's gift of love.

A relationship with God begins by admitting we are not perfect and continue to fall short of God's standards. Romans 3:23 says, "All have sinned and fall short of the glory of God." The price for these wrong-doings is separation from God. "The wages of sin is death, but the gift of God is eternal life in Christ Jesus our Lord" (Romans 6:23).

God's love comes to us right in the middle of our sin. "God proves His own love for us in that while we were still sinners Christ died for us!" (Romans 5:8). He doesn't ask us to clean up our lives first—in fact, without His help we are incapable of living by His standards.

Forgiveness begins when we admit our sin to God. When we do, He is faithful to forgive and restore our relationship with Him. "If we confess our sins, He is faithful and righteous to forgive us our sins and to cleanse us from all unrighteousness" (1 John 1:9).

Scripture confirms that this love gift and relationship with God are not just for a special few but for everyone. "Everyone who calls on the name of the Lord will be saved" (Romans 10:13). If you would like to receive God's gift of salvation, pray this prayer:

Dear God, I know that I am imperfect and separated from You. Please forgive me of my sin and adopt me as Your child. Thank You for this gift of life through the sacrifice of Your Son. I believe Jesus died for my sins. I will live my life for You. Amen.

If you prayed this prayer for the first time, share your experience with your small-group leader, your pastor, or a trusted Christian friend. To grow in your new life in Christ, continue to cultivate this new relationship through Bible study, prayer, and fellowship with other Christians. Welcome to God's family!

Leader Guide

This leader guide will help you facilitate six group sessions (plus an optional introductory session) for *The Frazzled Female*. The optional introductory session offers a time to distribute the workbooks and get acquainted. If you choose not to have an introductory session, make certain participants receive their workbooks in time to complete week 1 before group session 1.

Announce the study in the church newsletter, worship bulletin, on hallway bulletin boards, and at women's ministry activities.

Before each session, complete each week's assignments. As the leader you do not have to have all the answers, but you need to be familiar with the material. Don't feel you have to cover every activity in this leader guide. Many more discussion starters are offered each week than you will be able to cover in a single session. Be flexible. Consider the personality of your group as you make decisions about which topics to discuss. Allow the Lord to lead your group discussions.

INTRODUCTORY SESSION (OPTIONAL)

Before the Session
1. Read About the Author (p. 4) and About the Study (p. 5) and be prepared to introduce the author, the study, and the format.
2. Have copies of *The Frazzled Female* ready for distribution.
3. Prepare an attendance sheet for members to sign their names, addresses, phone numbers, and e-mail addresses. Place this sheet on a table with pens, markers, nametags, and a basket for collecting money.

During the Session
1. As participants arrive, ask them to sign in, prepare nametags, and pick up copies of the member book. If your church chooses to let group members pay for their workbooks, invite them to leave payment in the basket or offer to collect their money after the session.
2. Introduce yourself and, depending on the familiarity of the group, give a little information about yourself. Ask each member to do the same.
3. Briefly summarize the introductory material about the author. Draw attention to the About the Study page, and take some time to explain the unique elements of the study—the Defrazzler and Weekend Mini-Retreat. Encourage them to journal during the week about their experiences with these things and explain that they will have an opportunity to share their experiences each week in their group session.

4. Encourage members to share why they chose to participate in this study and what they anticipate happening in their lives as a result. Ask, *What frazzles you? How would you change your life to make it less frazzled?*

5. Remind everyone of the meeting times for each session. Emphasize the importance of individual study and group participation. Remind participants that everything discussed in your group will be kept confidential.

6. Assign week 1 for the next group session. Encourage them to complete each learning activity to get the most out of this study.

7. Ask God to give you an open heart as you commit to this study.

SESSION 1

Before the Session

1. If you did not have an introductory session, prepare the attendance sheet as directed in Before the Session for the optional introductory session. Place the attendance sheet, nametags, pencil or pens, and Bibles near the door. Have member books available for newcomers.

2. Complete the week 1 material.

During the Session

1. As participants arrive, ask them to sign in and prepare nametags.

2. If you did not have an introductory session, follow steps 2-5 in the optional introductory session suggestions.

3. Explain that each week you will discuss the material each person has studied individually during the week. Encourage them to complete every learning activity to get the most out of their study.

4. Draw their attention to the Totally Committed page (p. 112). Read through the commitment together, and ask participants to sign the page. Take a few minutes to let them sign each other's books as they commit to support other group members during the study.

5. Recite the week's memory verse (Matthew 6:33) together.

6. Use the following discussion starters:

   a. Talk about stepping back from some of the "good" things in our lives to experience the BEST thing, an intimate relationship with the Lord. Ask, *Are you working so hard for Him that you're bypassing your relationship with Him? How do you feel about getting to know Him better?* (p. 9)

   b. Discuss the choices Mary and Martha made about the time they spent with Jesus. Ask members to share ways they relate to each. Remind them of the two ways of "sitting at the feet of Jesus" discussed in day 2. Ask them to share which they most often practice. (p. 11)

c. Ask, *How often do you think about God during the day?* Ask a volunteer to read John 17:6-9. Talk about how it feels to know the Lord pursues a love relationship with you. Ask, *What things keep you from hearing God?* (p. 14)

d. Discuss how much God wants us to pour out our hearts to Him. Say, *He already knows the things that are in our hearts, but He wants us to talk to Him about them.* Encourage the ladies to spend some time during the next week sharing their deepest heart feelings with the Lord. Remind them that what God has in mind for us may not be what we have in mind, but what He has planned for our lives is always best!

e. Ask group members to break into groups of two or three and have someone in the group read Psalm 139:23-24. Instruct them to spend some time praying together, asking the Lord to show them anything in their lives that is interfering with their relationship with Him.

7. Invite members to share their experiences with the Defrazzler and the Weekend Mini-Retreat. If they need extra encouragement, you might want to share your experiences to get things started. As the group spends more time together, they will become more comfortable with sharing their experiences.

8. Close your time together in prayer, committing your study to God. Ask Him to help you make each week's individual study and participation in each small-group session a priority.

9. Assign week 2 for the next session.

SESSION 2

Before the Session

1. Complete the week 2 material.
2. Prepare the room for your group session. Place pencil or pens and Bibles near the door.
3. Have a chalkboard, poster board, or flipchart available.

During the Session

1. Welcome the ladies as they arrive.
2. Recite the week's memory verse (Proverbs 16:24) together.
3. Use these discussion starters:

a. Spend some time discussing Abraham's obedience to the Lord. Talk about making the choice to be obedient even when it doesn't "feel" good. Ask volunteers to share how they responded to the activity on page 24. Focus on how God blesses our obedience.

b. Talk about the importance of having a positive attitude—not just for ourselves but for others. Ask a volunteer to read Philippians 4:8. On a chalkboard, flipchart, or piece of poster board, brainstorm a list of the characteristics Paul tells us to think about. Next list specific actions we can take to stay positive (refer to the activity on page 27).

c. Discuss the importance of using God's power to make important changes in our attitudes. Ask, *What happens when you try to "do better" in your own strength?* Refer to the activities on page 30.

d. Ask, *How do we access God's power in our lives?* Briefly review the suggestions Cindi gave on pages 33-34. Ask group members if they tried any of these ideas, and, if so, how they worked for them.

e. Ask members how it makes them feel to know "God understands your inability and even your resistance to being positive when everything inside you feels negative. He knows that in your weakness you are not able to overlook all of life's negatives and immediately jump into a positive lifestyle." Explain, *He understands, and He wants us to rely on His power and the truth that He is God. He is in charge of our lives. What is our part in doing this? Our part is to believe—believe He is who He says He is and He will do what He says He will do!*

4. Invite the ladies to share their experiences with the Defrazzler and the Weekend Mini-Retreat. If they need some extra encouragement, share your experiences to get things started.

5. Close your time together in prayer. Ask God to help you utilize His power to help you be positive when it's easier to be negative.

6. Assign week 3 for the next session.

SESSION 3

Before the Session

1. Complete the week 3 material.
2. Prepare the room for your group session. Place pencil or pens and Bibles near the door.
3. Have a chalkboard, poster board, or flipchart available.

During the Session

1. Welcome the ladies as they arrive.
2. Recite the week's memory verse (John 14:1) together.
4. Use these discussion starters:

a. Refer to the learning activity on page 40. Ask them to share the activities they scored less than 5. Start a list on a chalkboard, flipchart, or poster board. Say, *Ask God if He wants you to spend more time on* these activities. If you feel He is saying yes, ask Him to show you how best to do this. If you don't feel Him urging the importance of these, ask Him to help you release any guilt you may be feeling about these areas.

b. Ask someone to read Matthew 6:19-21. Ask participants what they think it means to store up treasures in heaven. Ask them to name some ways they are doing this. Make a list on the board.

c. Ask for reactions to the comment, "God will not bless you in doing the things He has not called you to do." Ask group members if they were surprised by their level of commitment (or overcommitment) in the first activity on page 47. Ask for anyone who feels comfortable to share her response to the last activity on page 47.

d. Ask, *How often do you compare yourself to other women? Why do you think you are tempted to do that? Do you think that's what God wants us to do? Do you think the purpose of Proverbs 31 is to make us feel inadequate as godly women? How should we view this passage?*

e. Discuss things that cause you to feel overwhelmed and frustrated because there aren't enough hours in the day. Ask, *Is it time that's out of control, or are we out of control?* Encourage members to concentrate on what they do have control over (themselves) instead of what is beyond their control (circumstances).

5. Invite members to share their experiences with the Defrazzler and the Weekend Mini-Retreat. If they need extra encouragement, share your experiences to get things started.

6. Close in prayer. Ask God to be the God of your time.

7. Assign week 4 for the next session

SESSION 4

Before the Session

1. Complete the week 4 material.

2. Prepare the room for your group session. Place pencil or pens and Bibles near the door.

During the Session

1. Welcome the ladies as they arrive.

2. Recite the week's memory verse (Romans 12:18) together.

3. Use these discussion starters:

a. Talk about how the disciples must have felt when they learned of Jesus' departure. Ask members to share situations when they experienced similar feelings. Discuss the importance of recognizing our feelings without letting them shift our focus from the peace Jesus offers.

b. Ask a volunteer to read Romans 12:18. Remind members that our responsibility is to live at peace in every relationship. Encourage them to ask God to reveal someone who frustrates them—someone to whom they need to be especially kind. Ask, *What specific thing could you do to show love to someone who's not acting very lovable?"*

c. Ask a volunteer to read Romans 12:16-21. Ask group members if anyone identified a specific person in the activity at the top of page 62. If so, ask them if they were able to be an encouragement to that person. Did they see a difference in their relationship?

d. Talk about how difficult it can be to maintain a heavenly mindset when human emotions are aroused. Ask those who are comfortable doing so to share their responses to the activity on page 64. Ask, *What did God reveal to you this week to help you deal with "people" stress?*

e. Say, *In the day 5 material, Cindi shares some strategies she uses to help her deal with difficult people. Have you tried any of these? Do they work for you? Share your experiences.*

4. Invite members to share their experiences with the Defrazzler and the Weekend Mini-Retreat. If they need extra encouragement, share your experiences to get things started.

5. Close your time together in prayer. Ask God to help you keep you focus on Him instead of your circumstances. Pray that you will glorify Him in the way you treat difficult people.

6. Assign week 5 for the next session

SESSION 5

Before the Session

1. Complete the week 5 material.

2. Prepare the room for your group session. Place pencil or pens and Bibles near the door.

During the Session

1. Welcome the ladies as they arrive.

2. Recite the week's memory verse (Psalm 34:18) together.

3. Use these discussion starters:

a. Ask a volunteer to read 1 Corinthians 6:19. Ask group members how this verse impacts the way they view caring for their bodies. *In which areas (eating, sleeping, exercising, resting) do you need to set goals to help you better care for yourself? Spend some time this week seeking the Lord's guidance in how to best do this.*

b. "You are responsible for taking care of yourself by exercising, eating right, and getting enough sleep." (p. 74) Ask, *Do you agree with this statement?* If some members don't agree or are undecided, encourage discussion. Encourage members to use what they feel the Lord is telling them about taking care of themselves to set goals in the areas listed on page 76.

c. Share, *Being out of harmony with God can affect us emotionally, mentally, and physically. When we are involved in personal sin, God will allow us to experience great physical, emotional, and mental discomfort.* Read Psalm 32:3-4. Ask, *How can this discomfort be God's refining process, meant to draw us back to Him?* Take some time for group members to pray silently. Guide them to ask God to reveal any area in their lives that is causing a barrier in their relationship with Him. Encourage them to be obedient and accept His instruction.

d. Refer members to page 79. Ask, *Have you ever felt you didn't deserve God's love?* Encourage those who feel comfortable to describe their feelings about that time. Remind the ladies that we will never deserve the forgiveness of God. We can only accept and appreciate His forgiveness and be in awe of His extravagant love for us. Encourage them to praise Him for this love.

e. Ask group members how they would respond to the assignment to "Write a brief paragraph describing who you are." Ask, *How is your response different from how God views you? How does the reality of who you are in Christ change how you live your life?*

4. Invite members to share their experiences with the Defrazzler and the Weekend Mini-Retreat. If they need extra encouragement, share your experiences to get things started.

5. Close your time together in prayer. Ask God to show you what to do to best take care of your body, His temple. Thank Him that your true identity is in Him and not in any role you fill.

6. Assign week 6 for the next session

SESSION 6

Before the Session

1. Complete the week 6 material.

2. Prepare the room for your group session. Place pencil or pens and Bibles near the door.

3. Have a chalkboard, poster board, or flipchart available.

Special note to the leader: You will spend some time this week discussing depression. Your role is not that of a counselor but rather an encourager.

Watch for members who may be battling depression. Try to talk to them privately, and refer them to a doctor if they need to seek treatment. Let the Holy Spirit guide you through this sensitive subject.

During the Session

1. Welcome the ladies as they arrive.
2. Recite the week's memory verse (Acts 2:28) together.
3. Use these discussion starters:

   a. Discuss Peter's experience of walking on the water. Talk about how Peter had experienced and witnessed God's goodness but lost his focus during the storm. *In losing his focus, he lost sight of who he was in Jesus.* Ask for volunteers to share their experiences of allowing their focus to shift from Jesus to their circumstance. Compare Peter's reaction in the midst of the storm to Abraham's patience and obedience as he waited for God's promise to come to pass.

   b. Explain, *Being a Christian doesn't make you immune to difficulties.* Ask participants to share their response to: "Describe a circumstance in your life that you expected to be stress-free because of your relationship with the Lord." (p. 91) Ask a volunteer to read Psalm 34:18. Celebrate the Lord's promise to be close to the brokenhearted.

   c. Briefly discuss the symptoms of depression. Emphasize our responsibility to take care of ourselves and to seek help when we feel we have a problem. Remind them that God will reveal to us what we need to do and He'll give us the strength to do it. If anyone wants to share a testimony about dealing with depression, allow her to do so.

   d. Ask, *What events have made you flee the scene physically, mentally, or emotionally? What did you want God to do in your circumstance?* (p. 97) Discuss the importance of allowing God to minister to us, soothe us, and speak in His still, small voice. *Many times He will give us His presence instead of our desire of the moment.*

   e. Ask, *Have you ever considered that you are a love-gift to Jesus from the Father? Does this reality cause you to feel differently about your relationship with Jesus?* (pp. 100-101) *How does it make you feel to know Jesus prays to the Father for you?*

4. Invite members to share their experiences with the Defrazzler and the Weekend Mini-Retreat. If they need extra encouragement, share your experiences to get things started.

5. Close in prayer. Thank the Lord for always being near to the brokenhearted and for praying to the Father for you. Thank Him also for your time together as a group. Ask Him to help you be good stewards of the things you have learned during this study.

Two Ways to Earn Credit
for Studying LifeWay Christian Resources Material

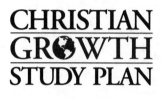

CHRISTIAN GROWTH STUDY PLAN

Christian Growth Study Plan resources are available for course credit for personal growth and church leadership training.

Courses are designed as plans for personal spiritual growth and for training current and future church leaders. To receive credit, complete the book, material, or activity. Respond to the learning activities or attend group sessions, when applicable, and show your work to your pastor, staff member, or church leader. Then go to *www.lifeway.com/CGSP*, or call the toll-free number for instructions for receiving credit and your certificate of completion.

For information about studies in the Christian Growth Study Plan, refer to the current catalog online at the CGSP Web address. This program and certificate are free LifeWay services to you.

CONTACT INFORMATION:
Christian Growth Study Plan
One LifeWay Plaza, MSN 117
Nashville, TN 37234
CGSP info line 1-800-968-5519
www.lifeway.com/CGSP
To order resources 1-800-458-2772

Need a CEU?

Receive Continuing Education Units (CEUs) when you complete group Bible studies by your favorite LifeWay authors.

Some studies are approved by the Association of Christian Schools International (ACSI) for CEU credits. Do you need to renew your Christian school teaching certificate? Gather a group of teachers or neighbors and complete one of the approved studies. Then go to *www.lifeway.com/CEU* to submit a request form or to find a list of ACSI-approved LifeWay studies and conferences. Book studies must be completed in a group setting. Online courses approved for ACSI credit are also noted on the course list. The administrative cost of each CEU certificate is only $10 per course.

CONTACT INFORMATION:
CEU Coordinator
One LifeWay Plaza, MSN 150
Nashville, TN 37234
Info line 1-800-968-5519
www.lifeway.com/CEU

LifeWay
Biblical Solutions for Life

Totally Committed

I, _____ commit
to my Father, my Bible study partners, and myself to:

1. Love the Lord with all my heart, soul, and mind.
2. Seek first His kingdom during the next six weeks.
3. Complete the weekly assignments before each group meeting.
4. Pray for the women in my group.
5. Keep the confidential matters discussed within the group session confidential.
6. Be open and obedient to the Holy Spirit's promptings.

Signature: _____

Signatures of group members:

_____

_____

_____

_____

_____

_____

_____

❀ ❀ ❀ ❀ ❀ ❀ ❀ ❀ ❀